Forgotten Treasures

Volume II

This collection first published in 2007 by
Express Newspapers
The Northern & Shell Building
10 Lower Thames Street
London EC3R 6EN

ISBN-13: 978-08507-9346-8

Cover design and typesetting by Susie Bell

Printed and bound in Poland. Produced by Polskabook

DAILY EXPRESS

Forgotten Treasures
Volume II

Compiled by
William Hartston

The Daily Express

Contents

Introduction

Since the publication of our first collection of *Forgotten Treasures* from the 'Forgotten Verse' column of the *Daily Express*, the flow of letters from readers has continued unabated. In total, we must now have received close to 10,000 requests, usually for poems learnt in childhood and now irritatingly returning to the memory in incomplete snatches. Sometimes, however, the requests have been for poems heard only once, which made a strong impression but have been elusive to track down.

The response to *Forgotten Treasures* has been extraordinary and heart-warming, with many readers writing to express their pleasure at having their favourite poems in book form. Remarkably, some were even asking when Book Two was coming out, even before the first one had been published! Poetry has a unique way of capturing our emotions, and the rediscovery of poems learnt at school seems to be a rejuvenating tonic for many. The following extract, from a letter sent to us by Wendy Bennett of Wakefield, is just one of many examples of the effect it can have:

'I gave one of the *Forgotten Treasures* books to my aunt, who is in her 90s and lives in a residential home. The staff say she's got a new lease of life. She spends many an afternoon regaling other patients with recitations from the book. I understand she does requests and has them in fits. So you've made several old people very happy!'

I think that says it all, and I hope this second book continues to bring great enjoyment.

William Hartston
Daily Express, **London, 2007**

1.

Inspirational

SOLITUDE
by Ella Wheeler Wilcox

Laugh, and the world laughs with you;
Weep, and you weep alone.
For the sad old earth must borrow its mirth,
But has trouble enough of its own.
Sing, and the hills will answer;
Sigh, it is lost on the air.
The echoes bound to a joyful sound,
But shrink from voicing care.

Rejoice, and men will seek you;
Grieve, and they turn and go.
They want full measure of all your pleasure,
But they do not need your woe.
Be glad, and your friends are many;
Be sad, and you lose them all.
There are none to decline your nectared wine,
But alone you must drink life's gall.

Feast, and your halls are crowded;
Fast, and the world goes by.
Succeed and give, and it helps you live,
But no man can help you die.
There is room in the halls of pleasure
For a long and lordly train,
But one by one we must all file on
Through the narrow aisles of pain.

Ella Wheeler Wilcox (1850–1919)

The poem was written by Wilcox in 1883 and was inspired by a train journey in New York on which the poet tried to comfort a woman sitting opposite her who was crying on her way to attend a funeral. It was first requested by Daniel Reid of Liverpool who, like so many of us, was familiar with the opening two lines but wanted to know what came next.

I KEEP SIX HONEST SERVING MEN
by Rudyard Kipling

I keep six honest serving men
(They taught me all I knew);
Their names are What and Why and When
And How and Where and Who.
I send them over land and sea,
I send them east and west;
But after they have worked for me,
I give them all a rest.

I let them rest from nine till five,
For I am busy then,
As well as breakfast, lunch and tea,
For they are hungry men.
But different folk have different views;
I know a person small –
She keeps ten million serving men,
Who get no rest at all!

She sends 'em abroad on her own affairs,
From the second she opens her eyes –
One million Hows, two million Wheres,
And seven million Whys!

Rudyard Kipling (1865–1936)
The first four lines of this poem are often quoted as a recommendation to keep up one's curiosity and willingness to ask questions, but few realise that there is more to the poem. This was requested by Ian Walker of Stoke-on-Trent who described it as 'a poem that I vaguely remember was around in the 1940s when I took my 11-plus exam.'

INVICTUS
by William Ernest Henley

Out of the night that covers me,
Black as the Pit from pole to pole,
I thank whatever gods may be
For my unconquerable soul.

In the fell clutch of circumstance
I have not winced nor cried aloud.
Under the bludgeonings of chance
My head is bloody, but unbowed.

Beyond this place of wrath and tears
Looms but the Horror of the shade,
And yet the menace of the years
Finds, and shall find, me unafraid.

It matters not how strait the gate,
How charged with punishments the scroll,
I am the master of my fate:
I am the captain of my soul.

William Ernest Henley (1849–1903)
This poem is said to have been written in praise of human resilience after Henley had one foot amputated, the result of a tuberculosis attack in his twenties. The poem was first requested by Pamela O'Callaghan from Cape Town, South Africa, who is one of many who recall the last two lines but cannot remember where they came from.

SAY NOT THE STRUGGLE
NAUGHT AVAILETH
by Arthur Hugh Clough

Say not the struggle naught availeth,
The labour and the wounds are vain,
The enemy faints not, nor faileth,
And as things have been, things remain.

If hopes were dupes, fears may be liars;
It may be, in yon smoke concealed,
Your comrades chase e'en now the fliers,
And, but for you, possess the field.

For while the tired waves, vainly breaking,
Seem here no painful inch to gain,
Far back through creeks and inlets making
Comes silent, flooding in, the main.

And not by eastern windows only,
When daylight comes, comes in the light,
In front the sun climbs slow, how slowly,
But westward, look, the land is bright.

Arthur Hugh Clough (1819–61)
Clough gave up a good teaching post at Oxford University to pursue his
inclinations to travel and write poetry. This verse was requested by
Mrs M A Leach of Bognor Regis who reminded us that Winston Churchill
used this poem in one of his rallying speeches in World War Two 'when we
were all a bit low'.

DUTY
by Elizabeth Barrett Browning

The sweetest lives are those to duty wed,
Whose deeds, both great and small,
Are close-knit strands of an unbroken thread,
There love ennobles all.
The world may sound no trumpet, ring no bells;
The book of life, the shining record tells.

Thy love shall chant its own beatitudes,
After its own life-working. A child's kiss
Set on thy singing lips shall make thee glad;
A poor man served by thee shall make thee rich;
A sick man helped by thee shall make thee strong;
Thou shalt be served thyself by every sense
Of service thou renderest.

Elizabeth Barrett Browning (1806–61)
To judge from the many requests we received for this poem, the opening line and the sentiment 'love ennobles all' stuck in many memories. Mrs E Simmonds of Birmingham recalled those lines from long-ago schooldays and summed up everyone's feelings: 'I remember the verse striking that delicate balance between nobility and sentimentality that all the best poetry aims for.'

OZYMANDIAS OF EGYPT
by Percy Bysshe Shelley

I met a traveller from an antique land
Who said: 'Two vast and trunkless legs of stone
Stand in the desert. Near them on the sand,
Half sunk, a shattered visage lies, whose frown
And wrinkled lip and sneer of cold command
Tell that its sculptor well those passions read
Which yet survive, stamped on these lifeless things,
The hand that mock'd them and the heart that fed;
And on the pedestal these words appear:
"My name is Ozymandias, king of kings:
Look on my works, ye Mighty, and despair!"
Nothing beside remains. Round the decay
Of that colossal wreck, boundless and bare,
The lone and level sands stretch far away.'

Percy Bysshe Shelley (1792–1822)
*Shelley was one of England's leading romantic poets and this verse is one of
his most popular. It has been requested by many readers, most of whom
remember the 'two vast and trunkless legs of sand' or 'My name is
Ozymandias', but the remainder is in general a blur.*

THE BUILDING OF THE SHIP
by Henry Wadsworth Longfellow

Thou, too, sail on, O Ship of State!
Sail on, O Union, strong and great!
Humanity with all its fears,
With all the hopes of future years,
Is hanging breathless on thy fate!
We know what Master laid thy keel,
What Workmen wrought thy ribs of steel,
Who made each mast, and sail, and rope,
What anvils rang, what hammers beat,
In what a forge and what a heat
Were shaped the anchors of thy hope!
Fear not each sudden sound and shock,
'Tis of the wave and not the rock;
'Tis but the flapping of the sail,
And not a rent made by the gale!
In spite of rock and tempest's roar,
In spite of false lights on the shore,
Sail on, nor fear to breast the sea
Our hearts, our hopes, are all with thee,
Our hearts, our hopes, our prayers, our tears,
Our faith triumphant o'er our fears,
Are all with thee, – are all with thee!

Henry Wadsworth Longfellow (1807–82)
This verse was prompted by a letter from Mrs B Williams who remembered singing the lines, 'Sail on, sail on, O Ship of State, Sail on, O Nation strong and great,' when she was at primary school during the Second World War. She asked, 'Could you tell me if this was from a speech by Winston Churchill? If not, who wrote it?' The poem is one section from a much longer work by Longfellow, and it did indeed play a part in one of Churchill's inspiring wartime speeches.

THE BLIND BOY
by Colley Cibber

O say what is that thing call'd Light,
    Which I must ne'er enjoy;
What are the blessings of the sight,
    O tell your poor blind boy!

You talk of wondrous things you see,
    You say the sun shines bright;
I feel him warm, but how can he
    Or make it day or night?

My day or night myself I make
    Whene'er I sleep or play;
And could I ever keep awake
    With me 'twere always day.

With heavy sighs I often hear
    You mourn my hapless woe;
But sure with patience I can bear
    A loss I ne'er can know.

Then let not what I cannot have
    My cheer of mind destroy:
Whilst thus I sing, I am a king,
    Although a poor blind boy.

Colley Cibber (1671–1757)
Colley Cibber was an extraordinary character who flourished in the first half of the eighteenth century. He saw himself as a serious actor and playwright, but attained greatest success when playing foppish characters in comedies. He became a successful actor/manager of the Drury Lane Theatre and, through his good personal contacts and astute politics, was created Poet Laureate in 1730, much to the disgust of several more worthy poets. Sheila Stubbs of Wolverhampton first requested this poem.

ELDORADO
by Edgar Allen Poe

Gaily bedight,
A gallant knight,
In sunshine and in shadow,
Had journeyed long,
Singing a song,
In search of Eldorado.

But he grew old –
This knight so bold –
And o'er his heart a shadow
Fell as he found
No spot of ground
That looked like Eldorado.

And, as his strength
Failed him at length,
He met a pilgrim shadow –
'Shadow,' said he,
'Where can it be –
This land of Eldorado?'

'Over the Mountains
Of the Moon,
Down the Valley of the Shadow,
Ride, boldly ride,'
The shade replied –
'If you seek for Eldorado!'

Edgar Allen Poe (1809–1849)
Brian Hughes of Leeds requested this poem: 'In a John Wayne film called El Dorado, *a character recites a poem with the line, "ride, boldly ride to the mountains of the moon". Was this written specially for the film?' The poem was actually written by Poe in the year he died.*

THE ARROW AND THE SONG
by Henry Wadsworth Longfellow

I shot an arrow into the air,
It fell to earth, I knew not where;
For, so swiftly it flew, the sight
Could not follow it in its flight.

I breathed a song into the air,
It fell to earth, I knew not where;
For who has sight so keen and strong,
That it can follow the flight of song?

Long, long afterward, in an oak
I found the arrow, still unbroke;
And the song, from beginning to end,
I found again in the heart of a friend.

Epic poems such as 'Hiawatha' earned Longfellow the status of America's National Poet, but as this shows, he could also produce highly effective short verse. Susan Andrews requested this poem: 'I shot an arrow in the air, it fell to earth I know not where – but what happened next? I have a feeling it killed someone, but cannot for the life of me remember.' We reassured Susan that the arrow hit a tree. It was the song accompanying it that struck home in Longfellow's delightful little poem.

THE THOUSANDTH MAN
by Rudyard Kipling

One man in a thousand, Solomon says,
    Will stick more close than a brother.
And it's worthwhile seeking him half your days
    If you find him before the other.
Nine hundred and ninety-nine depend
    On what the world sees in you,
But the Thousandth Man will stand your friend
    With the whole round world agin you.

'Tis neither promise nor prayer nor show
    Will settle the finding for 'ee.
Nine hundred and ninety-nine of 'em go
    By your looks, or your acts, or your glory.
But if he finds you and you find him
    The rest of the world don't matter;
For the Thousandth Man will sink or swim
    With you in any water.

You can use his purse with no more talk
    Than he uses yours for his spendings,
And laugh and meet in your daily walk
    As though there had been no lendings.
Nine hundred and ninety-nine of 'em call
    For silver and gold in their dealings;
But the Thousandth Man he's worth 'em all,
    Because you can show him your feelings.

His wrong's your wrong, his right's your right,
In season or out of season.
Stand up and back it in all men's sight –
With that for your only reason!
Nine hundred and ninety-nine can't bide
The shame or mocking or laughter,
But the Thousandth Man will stand by your side
To the gallows-foot – and after!

A gentle piece of wisdom from Kipling, written as though delivered by a father
or older man to a youngster, on the nature of true friendship and loyalty.

GOING DOWNHILL ON A BICYCLE
by Henry Charles Beeching

With lifted feet, hands still,
I am poised, and down the hill
Dart, with heedful mind;
The air goes by in a wind.

Swifter and yet more swift,
Till the heart with a mighty lift,
Makes the lungs laugh, the throat cry:
'O bird, see; see, bird, I fly.

'Is this, is this your joy?
O bird, then I, though a boy,
For a golden moment share
Your feathery life in air!'

Say, heart, is there aught like this
In a world that is full of bliss?
'Tis more than skating, bound
Steel-shod to the level ground.

Speed slackens now, I float
Awhile in my airy boat;
Till, when the wheels scarce crawl,
My feet to the treadles fall.

Alas, that the longest hill
Must end in a vale; but still,
Who climbs with toil, wheresoe'er,
Shall find wings waiting there.

Henry Charles Beeching (1859–1919)
Beeching was an English clergyman, author and poet who was, for some time,
Dean of Norwich. Valerie Evans of Farnborough remembered this poem from
a Christmas annual given to her as a child some seventy years ago.

2.

Romantic

THE BEGGAR MAID
by Alfred, Lord Tennyson

Her arms across her breast she laid;
She was more fair than words can say;
Barefooted came the beggar maid
Before the king Cophetua.

In robe and crown the king stept down,
To meet and greet her on her way;
It is no wonder, said the lords,
She is more beautiful than day.

As shines the moon in clouded skies,
She in her poor attire was seen;
One praised her ankles, one her eyes,
One her dark hair and lovesome mien.

So sweet a face, such angel grace,
In all that land had never been.
Cophetua swore a royal oath:
This beggar maid shall be my queen!

Alfred, Lord Tennyson (1809–92)
This poem by Tennyson was based on an old tale, mentioned by Shakespeare,
of a legendary king called Cophetua who showed no feelings towards women
until he met and fell in love with a beggar girl. The term 'Cophetua Complex'
has since been used to mean a love for lower-class women. Mrs C Charlesworth
of South Yorkshire first requested this poem; she remembered singing a
musical setting of it at school some sixty years ago. 'The only line I can recall,'
she admitted, 'is the last one: "This beggar maid shall be my queen".'

SONNET 18
William Shakespeare

Shall I compare thee to a Summer's day?
Thou art more lovely and more temperate:
Rough winds do shake the darling buds of May,
And Summer's lease hath all too short a date:
Sometime too hot the eye of heaven shines,
And often is his gold complexion dimm'd;
And every fair from fair sometime declines,
By chance or nature's changing course untrimm'd:
But thy eternal Summer shall not fade
Nor lose possession of that fair thou owest;
Nor shall Death brag thou wanderest in his shade,
When in eternal lines to time thou growest:
So long as men can breathe, or eyes can see,
So long lives this, and this gives life to thee.

William Shakespeare (1564–1616)
A few years ago, there was a highly successful television series called
The Darling Buds Of May, *but I wonder how many of the millions of*
viewers realised where the title originated? Curiously, the opening line is
perhaps the most quoted of all lines in the sonnets of William Shakespeare,
but few know how the poem continues.

SHE WALKS IN BEAUTY
by George Gordon, Lord Byron

She walks in beauty, like the night
Of cloudless climes and starry skies,
And all that's best of dark and bright
Meet in her aspect and her eyes,
Thus mellow'd to that tender light
Which heaven to gaudy day denies.

One shade the more, one ray the less,
Had half impair'd the nameless grace
Which waves in every raven tress
Or softly lightens o'er her face,
Where thoughts serenely sweet express
How pure, how dear their dwelling-place.

And on that cheek, and o'er that brow
So soft, so calm, yet eloquent,
The smiles that win, the tints that glow
But tell of days in goodness spent,
A mind at peace with all below,
A heart whose love is innocent.

George Gordon, Lord Byron (1788–1824)
Byron was the very model of a tragic romantic poet. Described by Lady Caroline Lamb as 'mad, bad and dangerous to know', his short life was a succession of romantic affairs and dangerous adventures. He kept a pet bear in his rooms in Cambridge, supposedly because Trinity College would not allow him a dog; he fought in revolutionary battles in Italy and Greece, and he wrote some of the most moving and memorable romantic poetry in the English language.

THE LOST LOVE
by William Wordsworth

She dwelt among the untrodden ways
Beside the springs of Dove;
A maid whom there were none to praise,
And very few to love.

A violet by a mossy stone
Half hidden from the eye!
Fair as a star, when only one
Is shining in the sky.

She lived unknown, and few could know
When Lucy ceased to be;
But she is in her grave, and O!
The difference to me!

William Wordsworth (1770–1850)
This is the second of five 'Lucy' poems by Wordsworth expressing the depth of his grief at the loss of a great love. The remarkable thing about the set is that the poet never tells us who Lucy is. A passionate mistress? A young child? Or even an imaginary symbol for perfect love itself? The intensity of the poet's feelings, though, is not in any doubt.

TO LUCASTA, ON GOING TO THE WARS
by Richard Lovelace

Tell me not, Sweet, I am unkind
That from the nunnery
Of thy chaste breast and quiet mind,
To war and arms I fly.

True, a new mistress now I chase,
The first foe in the field;
And with a stronger faith embrace
A sword, a horse, a shield.

Yet this inconstancy is such
As you too shalt adore;
I could not love thee, Dear, so much,
Loved I not Honour more.

Richard Lovelace (1618–59)

The royalist poet Richard Lovelace dedicated much of his verse to 'Lucasta', his pet name for Lucy Sacheverell. The tale of their romance had a sad ending: mistakenly believing him to have been killed at the Battle of Dunkirk in 1646, she married someone else. Born a nobleman, Lovelace spent his fortunes supporting the royalist cause and died in poverty at the age of forty. His brother published his poetry posthumously.

JENNY KISSED ME
by James Leigh Hunt

Jenny kissed me when we met,
Jumping from the chair she sat in;
Time, you thief, who love to get
Sweets into your list, put that in!
Say I'm weary, say I'm sad,
Say that health and wealth have missed me,
Say I'm growing old, but add,
Jenny kissed me.

James Leigh Hunt (1784–1859)
*Hunt was a leading figure, both as a poet and a publisher, among the
nineteenth-century Romantics. Indeed, it is said that it was at Hunt's house
that Shelley met Keats. The character of Harold Skimpole in Charles
Dickens's* Bleak House *was apparently based on him. This poem has been
frequently requested by readers, many of whom recall an early line or two,
but all remember the last line: 'Jenny kissed me'.*

LORD ULLIN'S DAUGHTER
by Thomas Campbell

A Chieftain, to the Highlands bound,
   Cries, 'Boatman, do not tarry!
And I'll give thee a silver pound
   To row us o'er the ferry!'

'Now, who be ye, would cross Lochgyle,
   This dark and stormy weather?'
   'O, I'm the chief of Ulva's isle,
And this, Lord Ullin's daughter.

'And fast before her father's men
   Three days we've fled together,
For should he find us in the glen,
   My blood would stain the heather.

'His horsemen hard behind us ride;
   Should they our steps discover,
Then who will cheer my bonny bride
   When they have slain her lover?'

Out spoke the hardy Highland wight,
   'I'll go, my chief, I'm ready:
It is not for your silver bright;
   But for your winsome lady:

'And by my word! the bonny bird
   In danger shall not tarry;
So, though the waves are raging white,
   I'll show you o'er the ferry.'

By this the storm grew loud apace,
   The water-wraith was shrieking;
And in the snowl of heaven each face
   Grew dark as they were speaking.

But still as wilder blew the wind,
And as the night grew drearer,
Adown the glen rode armèd men,
Their trampling sounded nearer.

'O haste thee, haste!' the lady cries,
'Though tempests round us gather;
I'll meet the raging of the skies,
But not an angry father.'

The boat has left a stormy land,
A stormy sea before her,
When, O! too strong for human hand,
The tempest gathere'd o'er her.

And still they row'd admidst the roar
Of waters fast prevailing:
Lord Ullin reach'd that fatal shore,
His wrath was changed to wailing.

For, sore dismay'd through storm and shade,
His child he did discover:
One lovely hand she stretch'd for aid,
And one was round her lover.

'Come back! come back!' he cried in grief
'Across this stormy water:
And I'll forgive your Highland chief,
My daughter! O my daughter!'

'Twas vain: the loud waves lash'd the shore,
Return or aid preventing:
The waters wild went o'er his child,
And he was left lamenting.

Thomas Campbell (1777–1844)
*This is a tragic and romantic tale of Highland elopement, written by one of
Scotland's leading nineteenth century poets.*

THE PASSIONATE SHEPHERD TO HIS LOVE
by Christopher Marlowe

Come live with me and be my Love,
And we will all the pleasures prove
That hills and valley, dale and field,
And all the craggy mountains yield.

There will we sit upon the rocks
And see the shepherds feed their flocks
By shallow rivers, to whose falls
Melodius birds sing madrigals.

There will make thee beds of roses
And a thousand fragrant posies,
A cap of flowers, and a kirtle
Embroider'd all with leaves of myrtle.

A gown made of the finest wool,
Which from our pretty lambs we pull,
Fair-lined slippers for the cold,
With buckles of the purest gold.

A belt of straw and ivy-buds
With coral clasps and amber studs:
And if these pleasures may thee move,
Come live with me and be my Love.

Thy silver dishes for thy meat
As precious as the gods do eat,
Shall on an ivory table be
Prepared each day for thee and me.

The shepherd swains shall dance and sing
For thy delight each May-morning:
If these delights thy mind may move,
Then live with me and be my Love.

Christopher Marlowe (1564–93)
This is a charming poem from Christopher Marlowe, with its wondrously effective romantic message sandwiched between the simple but effective opening and closing lines.

BALLAD OF EARL HALDAN'S DAUGHTER
by Charles Kingsley

It was Earl Haldan's daughter,
She looked across the sea;
She looked across the water
And long and loud laughed she:
'The locks of six princesses
Must be my marriage fee,
So hey bonny boat, ho bonny boat!
Who comes a wooing me?'

It was Earl Haldan's daughter,
She walked along the sand;
When she was aware of a knight so fair,
Came sailing to the land.
His sails were all of velvet,
His mast of beaten gold,
And 'Hey bonny boat, and ho bonny boat!
Who saileth here so bold?'

'The locks of five princesses
I won beyond the sea;
I clipt their golden tresses,
To fringe a cloak for thee.
One handful yet is wanting,
But one of all the tale;
So hey bonny boat, and ho bonny boat!
Furl up thy velvet sail!'

He leapt into the water,
That rover young and bold;
He gript Earl Haldan's daughter,
He clipt her locks of gold:
'Go weep, go weep, proud maiden,
The tale is full to-day.
Now hey bonny boat, and ho bonny boat!
Sail Westward ho! away!'

Charles Kingsley (1819–75)
This poem, which comes from Kingsley's novel Westward Ho! *was a dim, seventy-year-old memory for Mrs R. Green of Hull.*

A KISS
by Austin Dobson

Rose kissed me to-day.
Will she kiss me to-morrow?
Let it be as it may,
Rose kissed me to-day
But the pleasure gives way
To a savour of sorrow; –
Rose kissed me to-day, –
Will she kiss me to-morrow?

Henry Austin Dobson (1840–1921)

Henry Austin Dobson was a poet, essayist, biographer, and civil servant, who rose to the rank of Principal in the harbour department of the Board of Trade, evidently a job that left him enough time to indulge his passion for writing poetry.

R Martin of West London requested the poem via e-mail, saying that he had just been reminded of the poem after meeting a woman called Rose. We hope that finding the poem for him helped the relationship flourish. It's an example of a triolet – an eight-line verse of which the first, fourth and seventh lines are identical.

3.

Memories

LAY OF THE IMPRISONED HUNTSMAN
by Sir Walter Scott

My hawk is tired of perch and hood,
My idle greyhound loathes his food,
My horse is weary of his stall,
And I am sick of captive thrall.
I wish I were as I have been,
Hunting the hart in forest green,
With bended bow and bloodhound free,
For that's the life is meet for me.

I hate to learn the ebb of time
From yon dull steeple's drowsy chime,
Or mark it as the sunbeams crawl,
Inch after inch, along the wall.
The lark was wont my matins ring,
The sable rook my vespers sing;
These towers, although a king's they be,
Have not a hall of joy for me.

No more at dawning morn I rise,
And sun myself in Ellen's eyes,
Drive the fleet deer the forest through,
And homeward wend with evening dew;
A blithesome welcome blithely meet,
And lay my trophies at her feet,
While fled the eve on wing of glee,-
That life is lost to love and me!

Sir Walter Scott (1771–1832)
*Sheila Needham from Eastbourne set us on the trail of this poem with a
family reminiscence: 'When I went to school our English teacher instilled in us
a love of poetry. She gave us a poem to learn and when I showed it to my
father he told me he had learnt it at school as a song, and promptly sang it to
me. I have never been able to find the poem. Can you help?'*

YOUNG AND OLD
by Charles Kingsley

When all the world is young, lad,
And all the trees are green;
And every goose a swan, lad,
And every lass a queen;
Then hey for boot and horse, lad,
And round the world away;
Young blood must have its course, lad,
And every dog his day.

When all the world is old, lad,
And all the trees are brown;
And all the sport is stale, lad,
And all the wheels run down;
Creep home, and take your place there,
The spent and maimed among:
God grant you find one face there,
You loved when all was young.

We have frequent requests for poems by Charles Kingsley who is best known as the author of the children's classic The Water Babies. *This verse is from that very book, and can be found at the end of the second chapter. Mrs G Hunt from Port Talbot first requested this poem.*

SONG
by Christina Georgina Rossetti

When I am dead, my dearest,
  Sing no sad songs for me;
Plant thou no roses at my head,
  Nor shady cypress tree:
Be the green grass above me
With showers and dewdrops wet;
And if thou wilt, remember,
  And if thou wilt, forget.

I shall not see the shadows,
  I shall not feel the rain;
I shall not hear the nightingale
  Sing on, as if in pain;
And dreaming through the twilight
That doth not rise nor set,
Haply I may remember,
  And haply may forget.

Christina Rossetti (1830–94)
*Rossetti started writing poetry at the age of seven, but was already in her
thirties when her first collection,* Goblin Market and Other Poems, *was
published. When the book came out, the jacket featured an illustration by her
brother, the well-known painter Dante Gabriel Rossetti.*

WHEN I WAS ONE-AND-TWENTY
(from *A Shropshire Lad*)
by A E Housman

When I was one-and-twenty
I heard a wise man say,
'Give crowns and pounds and guineas
But not your heart away;
Give pearls away and rubies
But keep your fancy free.'
But I was one-and-twenty,
No use to talk to me.

When I was one-and-twenty
I heard him say again,
'The heart out of the bosom
Was never given in vain;
'Tis paid with sighs a plenty
And sold for endless rue.'
And I am two-and-twenty,
And oh, 'tis true, 'tis true.

Alfred Edward Housman (1859–1936)
*A E Housman was a brilliant classical scholar who went on to become
Professor of Latin at Cambridge. When not writing academic articles on
Latin and Greek authors, he put together a series of sixty-three poems under
the title A* Shropshire Lad, *of which the above is number thirteen and the
best known. Failing to find a publisher for the collection, he brought it out at
his own expense and they gradually became recognised as a major work of
English poetry.*

THE CHILD'S FIRST GRIEF
by Felicia Dorothea Hemans

'Oh! call my brother back to me,
I cannot play alone;
The summer comes with flower and bee –
Where is my brother gone?'

'The butterfly is glancing bright
Across the sunbeam's track;
I care not now to chase its flight –
Oh! call my brother back.'

'The flowers run wild – the flowers we sowed
Around our garden tree;
Our vine is drooping with its load –
Oh! call him back to me.'

'He would not hear my voice, fair child!
He may not come to thee;
The face that once like spring-time smiled
On earth no more thou'lt see.'

'A rose's brief, bright life of joy,
Such unto him was given;
Go – thou must play alone, my boy –
Thy brother is in heaven!'

'And has he left the birds and flowers,
And must I call in vain;
And through the long, long summer hours,
Will he not come again?'

'And by the brook, and in the glade,
Are all our wanderings o'er?
Oh! while my brother with me played,
Would I had loved him more!'

Felicia Dorothea Hemans (1793–1835)
Hemans is now best known for a single line of poetry: 'The boy stood on the burning deck', though in her time she had a large popular following.
    Patricia Gibson from Nottingham first requested this poem; she remembers her mother reciting it.

A MEETING
by Ella Wheeler Wilcox

Quite carelessly I turned the newsy sheet;
A song I sang, full many a year ago,
Smiled up at me, as in a busy street
One meets an old-time friend he used to know.

So full it was, that simple little song,
Of all the hope, the transport, and the truth,
Which to the impetuous morn of life belong,
That once again I seemed to grasp my youth.

So full it was of that sweet, fancied pain
We woo and cherish ere we meet with woe,
I felt as one who hears a plaintive strain
His mother sang him in the long ago.

Up from the grave the years that lay between
That song's birthday and my stern present came
Like phantom forms and swept across the scene,
Bearing their broken dreams of love and fame.

Fair hopes and bright ambitions that I knew
In that old time, with their ideal grace,
Shone for a moment, then were lost to view
Behind the dull clouds of the commonplace.

With trembling hands I put the sheet away;
   Ah, little song! the sad and bitter truth
Struck like an arrow when we met that day!
My life has missed the promise of its youth.

This poem is a wonderful evocation of the mixture of joy and sadness that memories of one's early years can bring. A Richards of Oxford requested this poem, having remembered only the telling final line: 'My life has missed the promise of its youth'.

A FAREWELL
by Charles Kingsley

My fairest child, I have no song to give you;
No lark could pipe to skies so dull and gray:
Yet, ere we part, one lesson I can leave you
For every day.

Be good, sweet maid, and let who will be clever;
Do noble things, not dream them, all day long:
And so make life, death, and that vast forever
One grand, sweet song.

The choice of this poem stemmed from an entry in a school autograph book. Jean Hibbs from Haverfordwest wrote: 'When I left school in Hammersmith at the age of fourteen years (that's seventy-six years ago), my English teacher entered a verse in my autograph book, beginning: "Go forth sweet maid, let who will be clever, Do noble things not dream them all day long." I have never heard this since. Is there any more to it, or was it her own effort?'

AT NIGHT
by Alice Meynell

Home, home from the horizon far and clear,
   Hither the soft wings sweep;
Flocks of the memories of the day draw near
   The dovecote doors of sleep.
O which are they that come through sweetest light
   Of all these homing birds?
Which with the straightest and the swiftest flight?
   Your words to me, your words!

Alice Meynell (1847–1922)
Meynell was, when not looking after her eight children, a poet, magazine editor and campaigner for votes for women. She died in 1922 at the age of seventy-five. This poem was requested by Audrey Thorn, of Dover, who remembers having learnt at school, sixty-five years ago, 'a poem about our experiences of the day coming into our minds at night like a flock of birds coming home to roost'.

PAST AND PRESENT
by Thomas Hood

I remember, I remember
The house where I was born,
The little window where the sun
Came peeping in at morn;
He never came a wink too soon
Nor brought too long a day;
But now, I often wish the night
Had borne my breath away.

I remember, I remember
The roses, red and white,
The violets, and the lilycups
Those flowers made of light!
The lilacs where the robin built,
And where my brother set
The laburnum on his birthday,
The tree is living yet!

I remember, I remember
Where I was used to swing,
And thought the air must rush as fresh
To swallows on the wing;
My spirit flew in feathers then
That is so heavy now,
And summer pools could hardly cool
The fever on my brow.

I remember, I remember
The fir-trees dark and high;
I used to think their slender tops
Were close against the sky:
It was a childish ignorance,
But now 'tis little joy
To know I'm farther off from Heaven
Than when I was a boy.

Thomas Hood (1799–1845)
_Hood was a London humorist and poet and this verse is peculiarly
appropriate for a collection of forgotten verse. To judge from the many
requests we have received, everyone remembers 'I remember, I remember',
but few memories stretch beyond 'the house where I was born'._

THE SANDS OF DEE
by Charles Kingsley

'O Mary, go and call the cattle home,
And call the cattle home,
And call the cattle home,
Across the sands of Dee!'
The western wind was wild and dank with foam
And all alone went she.

The western tide crept up along the sand,
And o'er and o'er the sand,
And round and round the sand,
As far as eye could see.
The rolling mist came down and hid the land;
And never home came she.

Oh! is it weed, or fish, or floating hair,-
A tress of golden hair,
A drownèd maiden's hair,
Above the nets at sea?
Was never salmon yet that shone so fair
Among the stakes on Dee.

They rowed her in across the rolling foam,
The cruel crawling foam,
The cruel hungry foam,
To her grave beside the sea.
But still the boatmen hear her call the cattle home
Across the sands of Dee.

This verse has been frequently requested, including a plea by Pamela Long of Guernsey, who wrote: 'Sixty years ago, I can remember my mother reciting to me a verse beginning "Mary call the cattle home". I would be so grateful if you could find the rest of the poem.'

PETRA
by John William Burgon

O passing beautiful in this wild spot
Temples, and tombs, and dwellings, all forgot!
One sea of sunlight far around them spread,
And skies of sapphire mantling overhead.
They seem no work of man's creative hand,
Where Labour wrought as wayward Fancy plann'd;
But from the rock as if by magic grown,
Eternal – silent – beautiful – alone!
Not virgin white like that old Doric shrine
Where once Athena held her rites divine:
Not saintly grey like many a minster fane
That crowns the hill, or sanctifies the plain:
But rosy-red, as if the blush of dawn
Which first beheld them were not yet withdrawn:
The hues of youth upon a brow of woe,
Which men call'd old two thousand years ago!
Match me such marvel, save in Eastern clime,
A rose-red city – half as old as Time!

John William Burgon (1813–88)
John William Burgon was Professor of Divinity at Oxford and wrote this poem in 1845, celebrating the discovery, thirty-three years earlier, of the lost city of Petra in Jordan. Burgon finally visited Petra in 1862 when he announced that he'd got the colour wrong: 'There is nothing rosy in Petra by any means.'

Gwynneth McCullock asked, 'Please, could you find a poem that I read many years ago. The only line I remember is "rose-red city half as old as time".'

CROSSING THE BAR
by Alfred, Lord Tennyson

Sunset and evening star,
And one clear call for me!
And may there be no moaning of the bar,
When I put out to sea,

But such a tide as moving seems asleep,
Too full for sound and foam,
When that which drew from out the boundless deep
Turns home again.

Twilight and evening bell,
And after that the dark!
And may there be no sadness or farewell,
When I embark;

For tho' from out our bourne of Time and Place
The flood may bear me far,
I hope to see my Pilot face to face
When I have crost the bar.

Tennyson had a special request associated with this poem: he wrote it some three years before he died and, though he wrote several poems in those years, he asked that 'Crossing the Bar' always should be the last poem in any collection of his work. Likening sunset and the rise of the evening star to the author's impending demise, the poem reflects his coming to terms with his own mortality. Mrs M Lindsay of Glasgow requested this poem.

4.

Spiritual

BALLAD OF THE TEMPEST
by James Thomas Fields

We were crowded in the cabin,
Not a soul would dare to sleep,
It was midnight on the waters,
And a storm was on the deep.

'Tis a fearful thing in winter
To be shattered by the blast,
And to hear the rattling trumpet
Thunder, 'Cut away the mast!'

So we shuddered there in silence,
For the stoutest held his breath,
While the hungry sea was roaring
And the breakers talked with Death.

As thus we sat in darkness,
Each one busy with his prayers,
'We are lost!' the captain shouted
As he staggered down the stairs.

But his little daughter whispered,
As she took his icy hand,
'Isn't God upon the ocean,
Just the same as on the land?'

Then we kissed the little maiden.
　And we spoke in better cheer,
And we anchored safe in harbour
When the morn was shining clear.

James Thomas Fields (1817–81)
Fields was an American publisher, magazine editor and essayist who also wrote some very accessible and popular poetry. The lines most frequently quoted from the poem above are '"We are lost!" the captain shouted, As he staggered down the stairs', though the couplet that stuck in the memory of Sylvia Davies from Newport, Gwent, which led to her request, was: 'Isn't God upon the ocean, just the same as on the land?'

AMAZING GRACE
by John Newton

Amazing grace! (how sweet the sound)
That sav'd a wretch like me!
I once was lost, but now am found,
Was blind, but now I see.

'Twas grace that taught my heart to fear,
And grace my fears reliev'd;
How precious did that grace appear,
The hour I first believ'd!

Thro' many dangers, toils and snares,
I have already come;
'Tis grace has brought me safe thus far,
And grace will lead me home.

The Lord has promis'd good to me,
His word my hope secures;
He will my shield and portion be,
As long as life endures.

Yes, when this flesh and heart shall fail,
And mortal life shall cease;
I shall possess, within the veil,
A life of joy and peace.

The earth shall soon dissolve like snow,
The sun forbear to shine;
But God, who call'd me here below,
Will be forever mine.

John Newton (1725–1807)
*'Amazing Grace' began life as a hymn written by Newton, shipmaster,
press-ganged sailor, slave trader and finally evangelical preacher following
his conversion in 1748 after praying for salvation during a storm at sea. Mrs
H Price of Bridgend first requested this poem.*

CHILDREN'S PRAYER
by Adelheid Wette

When at night I go to sleep
Fourteen angels watch do keep;
Two my head are guarding,
Two my feet are guiding;
Two are on my right hand,
Two are on my left hand,
Two who warmly cover
Two who o'er me hover,
Two to whom 'tis given
To guide my steps to heaven.

Sleeping sofly, then it seems
Heaven enters in my dreams;
Angels hover round me,
Whisp'ring they have found me;
Two are sweetly singing,
Two are garlands bringing,
Strewing me with roses
As my soul reposes.
God will not forsake me
When dawn at last will wake me.

Adelheid Wette (1858–1916)
The verse comes from Engelbert Humperdinck's opera Hansel and Gretel.
Adelheid Wette, Humperdinck's sister, wrote the original libretto. This is the English translation.

Mrs Carey Bromwell of Rickmansworth, Hertfordshire, requested this poem for a rather surprising reason: 'When I had a number of cats, they used to come up on my bed and remind me of the lines "when at night I go to sleep, fourteen angels watch do keep". I'd love to be reminded of the rest of it.'

5.

Narrative

EXCELSIOR!
by Henry Wadsworth Longfellow

The shades of night were falling fast,
As through an Alpine village passed
A youth, who bore, mid snow and ice,
A banner with the strange device
Excelsior!

His brow was sad; his eye beneath
Flashed like a falchion from its sheath;
And like a silver clarion rung
The accents of that unknown tongue
Excelsior!

In happy homes he saw the light
Of household fires gleam warm and bright,
Above, the spectral glaciers shone,
And from his lips escaped a groan
Excelsior!

'Try not the pass,' the old man said:
'Dark lowers the tempest overhead;
The roaring torrent is deep and wide.'
And loud that clarion voice replied,
Excelsior!

'Oh, stay,' the maiden said, 'and rest
Thy weary head upon this breast!'
A tear stood in his bright blue eye,
But still he answered with a sigh,
Excelsior!

'Beware the pine-tree's withered branch!
Beware the awful avalanche!'
This was the peasant's last Good-night:
A voice replied, far up the height:
Excelsior!

At break of day, as heavenward
The pious monks of Saint Bernard
Uttered the oft-repeated prayer,
A voice cried through the startled air,
Excelsior!

A traveller, by the faithful hound,
Half-buried in the snow was found,
Still grasping in his hand of ice
That banner with the strange device,
Excelsior!

There in the twilight, cold and gray,
Lifeless, but beautiful, he lay,
And from the sky, serene and far,
A voice fell, like a falling star
Excelsior!

A reference to pious monks, a traveller on a mountain, and a slogan that was also the title of the poem, was all that Gordon McAlorian from Carrickfergus could remember from having seen this poem sixty-five years ago at school. It is a typically stirring piece from the pen of America's greatest poet of the nineteenth century, Longfellow.

THE CHILDREN'S HOME
by F E Weatherly

They played, in their beautiful garden,
The children of high degree;
Outside the gate the beggars
Passed on in their misery!
But there was one of the children
Who could not join in their play,
And a little beggar maiden
Watched for him day by day.

Once he had given her a flower,
And oh! how he smiled to see
Her thin white hand through the railing,
Stretched out so eagerly.
She came again to the garden,
She watched the childlren play,
But the little white face had vanished,
The little feet gone away.

She crept away to her comer,
Down by the murky stream,
But the pale face in the garden
Shone through her restless dream.
And that pale-faced child and the beggar
Passed homeward side by side;
For the ways of men are narrow,
But the gates of heaven are wide!

Frederick Edward Weatherley (1848–1929)
Weatherley was an English lawyer who also wrote poetry and song lyrics.
This is probably his best-known work and was requested by Mrs D M Dawe
of Rushden, Northants, who told us she learnt it at school seventy-five years
ago: 'Our teacher thought it was a beautiful poem, but now it sounds
positively twee and sentimental,' she says.

O CAPTAIN! MY CAPTAIN!
by Walt Whitman

O Captain! My Captain! our fearful trip is done,
The ship has weathered every rack, the prize we sought is won;
The port is near, the bells I hear, the people all exulting,
While follow eyes the steady keel, the vessel grim and daring;
But, O heart! heart! heart!
O the bleeding drops of red,
Where on the deck my Captain lies,
Fallen, cold and dead.

O Captain! My Captain! rise up and hear the bells;
Rise up – for you the flag is flung – for you the bugle trills,
For you bouquets and ribboned wreaths – for you the shores
a-crowding,
For you they call, the swaying mass, their eager faces turning;
Here Captain! dear father!
This arm beneath your head!
It is some dream that on the deck
You've fallen cold and dead.

My Captain does not answer, his lips are pale and still;
My father does not feel my arm, he has no pulse or will;
The ship is anchored safe and sound, its voyage closed and done;
From fearful trip the victor ship comes in with object won;
Exult, O shores! and ring, O bells!
But I, with mournful tread,
Walk the deck my Captain lies,
Fallen, cold and dead.

Walt Whitman (1819–92)
In the film Dead Poets' Society, *Robin Williams asks his pupils to address
him as 'O Captain, my Captain'. Several readers asked for the complete poem
from which he took the line. Walt Whitman is said to have written it originally
in memory of Abraham Lincoln.*

FENCE OR AMBULANCE?
by Joseph Malins

'Twas a dangerous cliff, as they freely confessed,
Though to walk near its crest was so pleasant;
But over its terrible edge there had slipped
A duke and full many a peasant.
So the people said something would have to be done,
But their projects did not at all tally;
Some said, 'Put a fence 'round the edge of the cliff,'
Some, 'An ambulance down in the valley.'

But the cry for the ambulance carried the day,
For it spread through the neighbouring city;
A fence may be useful or not, it is true,
But each heart became full of pity
For those who slipped over the dangerous cliff;
And the dwellers in highway and alley
Gave pounds and gave pence, not to put up a fence,
But an ambulance down in the valley.

'For the cliff is all right, if you're careful,' they said,
'And, if folks even slip and are dropping,
It isn't the slipping that hurts them so much
As the shock down below when they're stopping.'
So day after day, as these mishaps occurred,
Quick forth would those rescuers sally
To pick up the victims who fell off the cliff,
With their ambulance down in the valley.

Then an old sage remarked: 'It's a marvel to me
That people give far more attention
To repairing results than to stopping the cause,
When they'd much better aim at prevention.
Let us stop at its source all this mischief,' cried he.
'Come, neighbours and friends, let us rally;
If the cliff we will fence, we might almost dispense
With the ambulance down in the valley.'

'Oh he's a fanatic,' the others rejoined,
'Dispense with the ambulance? Never!
He'd dispense with all charities, too, if he could;
No! No! We'll support them forever.
Aren't we picking up folks just as fast as they fall?
And shall this man dictate to us? Shall he?
Why should people of sense stop to put up a fence,
While the ambulance works in the valley?'

But the sensible few, who are practical too,
Will not bear with such nonsense much longer;
They believe that prevention is better than cure,
And their party will soon be the stronger.
Encourage them then, with your purse, voice, and pen,
And while other philanthropists dally,
They will scorn all pretense, and put up a stout fence
On the cliff that hangs over the valley.

Better guide well the young than reclaim them when old,
For the voice of true wisdom is calling.
'To rescue the fallen is good, but 'tis best
To prevent other people from falling.'
Better close up the source of temptation and crime
Than deliver from dungeon or galley;
Better put a strong fence 'round the top of the cliff
Than an ambulance down in the valley.

Joseph Malins (1844–1926)
*Malins was born in England but spent much of his early life in America,
where he was a leading campaigner against alcohol. This poem was in fact
written as an argument for the prohibition of alcohol, prevention being better
than cure. Eileen O'Dwyer, who had a tale of regret at not having bought a
tea-towel, requested the poem: 'I only saw this poem once, printed on a tea
towel. I wish I had bought one now!' she said.*

THE VOLUNTEER ORGANIST
by William B Gray

The preacher in the village church one Sunday morning said:
'Our organist is ill today, will someone play instead?'
An anxious look crept o'er the face of ev'ry person there
As eagerly they watched to see who'd fill the vacant chair.

A man then staggered down the aisle, whose clothes were old and torn
How strange a drunkard seem'd to me in church on Sunday morn,
But as he touched the organ keys, without a single word
The melody that followed was the sweetest ever heard.

Each eye shed tears within that church, the strongest men grew pale,
The organist in melody had told his own life's tale,
The sermon of the preacher was no lesson to compare
With that of life's example, who sat in the organ chair.

And when the service ended, not a soul had left a seat,
Except the poor old organist who started toward the street
Along the aisle and out the door he slowly walked away,
The preacher rose and softly said: 'Good brethren, let us pray.'

The scene was one I'll ne'er forget as long as I may live,
And just to see it o'er again all earthly wealth I'd give.
The congregation all amazed, the preacher old and grey,
The organ and the organist who volunteered to play.

William B Gray (dates unknown)
This verse is, in fact, a song lyric, first published in 1893. Georgina Baron of Bristol requested it, telling us, 'When I was twenty-one years old and a WAAF stationed at RAF Amport in Hampshire, this was sung or recited to me by Sid, our civilian cook. I am now seventy-seven, but the thought of this verse still makes me cry.'

6.

Nature

A BOY'S SONG
by James Hogg

Where the pools are bright and deep,
Where the grey trout lies asleep,
Up the river and over the lea,
That's the way for Billy and me.

Where the blackbird sings the latest,
Where the hawthorn blooms the sweetest,
Where the nestlings chirp and flee,
That's the way for Billy and me.

Where the mowers mow the cleanest,
Where the hay lies thick and greenest,
There to track the homeward bee,
That's the way for Billy and me.

Where the hazel bank is steepest,
Where the shadow falls the deepest,
Where the clustering nuts fall free,
That's the way for Billy and me.

Why the boys should drive away
Little sweet maidens from the play,
Or love to banter and fight so well,
That's the thing I never could tell.

But this I know, I love to play
Through the meadow, among the hay;
Up the water and over the lea,
That's the way for Billy and me.

James Hogg (1770–1835)

James Hogg – a novelist and poet – lived and worked for most of his life in Ettrick Forest on the Scottish borders. There is even a statue of him standing by St Mary's Loch in Scotland.

Jean Fraser of Inverness, who requested the poem, told us she had been trying to find it for more than twenty years. 'I feel that you are my very last hope,' she wrote. 'It was in a primary school book we had in the Sixties when I was only seven or eight. The poem was about a boy and his friend having a great play in a field. I did love that poem, but I don't know who wrote it.'

THE SEA
by Barry Cornwall

The sea! the sea! the open sea!
The blue, the fresh, the ever free!
Without a mark, without a bound,
It runneth the earth's wide regions round;
It plays with the clouds; it mocks the skies;
Or like a cradled creature lies.

I'm on the sea! I'm on the sea!
I am where I would ever be;
With the blue above, and the blue below,
And silence wheresoe'er I go;
If a storm should come and awake the deep,
What matter? I shall ride and sleep.

I love, O, how I love to ride
On the fierce, foaming, bursting tide,
When every mad wave drowns the moon
Or whistles aloft his tempest tune,
And tells how goeth the world below,
And why the sou'west blasts do blow.

I never was on the dull, tame shore,
But I lov'd the great sea more and more,
And backwards flew to her billowy breast,
Like a bird that seeketh its mother's nest;
And a mother she was, and is, to me;
For I was born on the open sea!

The waves were white, and red the morn,
  In the noisy hour when I was born;
And the whale it whistled, the porpoise roll'd,
And the dolphins bared their backs of gold;
  And never was heard such an outcry wild
  As welcom'd to life the ocean-child!

I've liv'd since then, in calm and strife,
  Full fifty summers, a sailor's life,
With wealth to spend and a power to range,
But never have sought nor sighed for change;
  And Death, whenever he comes to me,
  Shall come on the wild, unbounded sea!

Bryan Wallace Procter (1787–1874)
Barry Cornwall was the pseudonym of Bryan Waller Procter, a lawyer who served for thirty years as metropolitan commissioner of lunacy.

  Ethel Lord from Rossendale, Lancs, requested this poem, with a memory of her schooldays: 'The lady who taught us poetry sixty years ago was stone deaf, but she managed to get it over to us, and I have never forgotten them entirely.'

DAFFODILS
by William Wordsworth

I wandered lonely as a Cloud
That floats on high o'er Vales and Hills,
When all at once I saw a crowd,
A host of golden daffodils;
Beside the lake, beneath the trees,
Fluttering and dancing in the breeze.

Continuous as the stars that shine
And twinkle on the milky way,
They stretched in never-ending line
Along the margin of a bay:
Ten thousand saw I at a glance,
Tossing their heads in sprightly dance.

The waves beside them danced, but they
Out-did the sparkling waves in glee:-
A poet could not but be gay
In such a jocund company:
I gazed – and gazed – but little thought
What wealth the show to me had brought:

For oft when on my couch I lie
In vacant or in pensive mood,
They flash upon that inward eye
Which is the bliss of solitude,
And then my heart with pleasure fills,
And dances with the Daffodils.

This poem is a real classic, requested by Barbara Lyons of London, Ontario, in Canada. Asking for 'a host of golden daffodils' she wrote: 'I tried to remember this poem, which I had to recite on stage when I was at school. I would like my grandchildren to learn it as it so reminds me of my homeland, England.'

THE BROOK
by Alfred, Lord Tennyson

I chatter, chatter, as I flow
To join the brimming river;
For men may come and men may go,
But I go on forever.

I wind about, and in and out,
With here a blossom sailing,
And here and there a lusty trout,
And here and there a grayling.

I steal by lawns and grassy plots,
I slide by hazel covers;
I move the sweet forget-me-nots
That grow for happy lovers.

I slip, I slide, I gloom, I glance,
Among my skimming swallows;
I make the netted sunbeams dance
Against my sandy shallows.

I murmur under moon and stars
In brambly wildernesses;
I linger by my shingly bars;
I loiter round my cresses.

And out again I curve and flow
To join the brimming river;
For men may come and men may go,
But I go on forever.

Tennyson was Poet Laureate and a master of epic verse on the themes of mythology or legend. Verses such as 'The Brook' show his talent at matching the rhythms of the words to the rhythms of nature. This is only an extract from what is a much longer poem.

FORGET-ME-NOT
by Emily Bruce Roelofson

When to the flowers so beautiful
The Father gave a name,
Back came a little blue-eyed one
(All timidly it came);
And standing at its Father's feet
And gazing in His face,
It said, in low and trembling tone
And with a modest grace,
'Dear God, the name Thou gavest me,
Alas I have forgot!'
Kindly the Father looked him down
And said: 'Forget-me-not.'

Emily Bruce Roelofson (dates unknown)
Emily Bruce Roelefson was an American poet and song-writer of the late nineteenth century.

Sarah Gordon of Glasgow wrote to us hoping to be reunited with a poem that was her party piece more than sixty years ago. 'It was about God giving names to all the flowers. One of them forgot, and the line I remember is "Back came a little blue-eyed one".'

TO DAFFODILS
by Robert Herrick

Fair Daffodils, we weep to see
You haste away so soon:
As yet the early-rising Sun
Has not attain'd his noon.
Stay, stay,
Until the hasting day
Has run
But to the even-song;
And, having pray'd together, we
Will go with you along.

We have short time to stay, as you,
We have as short a Spring;
As quick a growth to meet decay
As you, or any thing.
We die,
As your hours do, and dry
Away
Like to the Summer's rain;
Or as the pearls of morning's dew
Ne'er to be found again.

Robert Herrick (1591–1674)
*Robert Herrick wrote some of the most romantic poetry in the English
language but died a bachelor at the age of eighty-three.*

*The above poem, requested by Mrs O Broicher of Kingskerswell, Devon,
is a nice reminder that Wordsworth was not the first to write about daffodils.*

THE NIGHT WIND
by Eugene Field

Have you ever heard the wind go 'Yooooo'?
　　'Tis a pitiful sound to hear!
It seems to chill you through and through
　　With a strange and speechless fear.
'Tis the voice of the night that broods outside
　　When folk should be asleep,
And many and many's the time I've cried
To the darkness brooding far and wide
　　Over the land and the deep:
'Whom do you want, O lonely night,
　　That you wail the long hours through?'
And the night would say in its ghostly way:
　　　　'Yoooooooo!
　　　　Yoooooooo!
　　　　Yoooooooo!'

My mother told me long ago
　　(When I was a little tad)
That when the night went wailing so,
　　Somebody had been bad;
And then, when I was snug in bed,
　　Whither I had been sent,
With the blankets pulled up round my head,
I'd think of what my mother'd said,
　　And wonder what boy she meant!
And 'Who's been bad to-day?' I'd ask
　　Of the wind that hoarsely blew,
And the voice would say in its meaningful way:
　　　　'Yoooooooo!
　　　　Yoooooooo!
　　　　Yoooooooo!'

That this was true I must allow –
You'll not believe it, though!
Yes, though I'm quite a model now,
I was not always so.
And if you doubt what things I say,
Suppose you make the test;
Suppose, when you've been bad some day
And up to bed are sent away
From mother and the rest –
Suppose you ask, 'Who has been bad?'
And then you'll hear what's true;
For the wind will moan in its ruefullest tone:
'Yoooooooo!
Yoooooooo!
Yoooooooo!'

Eugene Field (1850–95)
Eugene Field was an American journalist who became best known for his
light and humorous poems for children, of which the above is a typical
example.

COME LITTLE LEAVES
by George Cooper

Come, little leaves, said the wind one day
Come o'er the meadows with me and play
Put on your dresses of red and gold
For summer is gone and the days grow cold.

Soon as the leaves heard the wind's loud call
Down they came fluttering, one and all
Over the brown fields they danced and flew
Singing the glad little songs they knew.

Cricket, goodbye, we've been friends so long
Little brook, sing us your farewell song
Say you are sorry to see us go
Ah, you will miss us, right well we know.

Dear little lambs in your fleecy fold
Mother will keep you from harm and cold
Fondly we watched you in vale and glade
Say, will you dream of our loving shade?

Dancing and whirling, the little leaves went
Winter had called them, and they were content
Soon, fast asleep in their earthy beds
The snow laid a coverlet over their heads.

George Cooper (1820–76)
Marion Reed of Romsey, Hants, who remembered her mother reciting it to
her as a child, first requested this autumnal verse: 'Mum would stand with her
hands to show how the leaves fluttered.'

WHEN ICICLES HANG BY THE WALL
by William Shakespeare

When icicles hang by the wall,
And Dick the shepherd blows his nail,
And Tom bears logs into the hall,
And milk comes frozen home in pail,
When blood is nipp'd and ways be foul,
Then nightly sings the staring owl,
Tu-whit; Tu-who, a merry note,
While greasy Joan doth keel the pot.

When all aloud the wind doth blow,
And coughing drowns the parson's saw,
And birds sit brooding in the snow,
And Marian's nose looks red and raw,
When roasted crabs hiss in the bowl,
Then nightly sings the staring owl,
Tu-whit; Tu-who, a merry note,
While greasy Joan doth keel the pot.

We have had many requests for this poem. Some remember the opening line, others recall greasy Joan keeling the pot, but surprisingly few remember that it is by Shakespeare. The verse is sung in the fifth act of Love's Labour's Lost.

WEATHERS
by Thomas Hardy

This is the weather the cuckoo likes,
        And so do I;
When showers betumble the chestnut spikes,
        And nestlings fly;
And the little brown nightingale bills his best,
And they sit outside at 'The Traveller's Rest',
And maids come forth sprig-muslin drest,
And citizens dream of the south and west,
        And so do I.

This is the weather the shepherd shuns,
        And so do I;
When beeches drip in browns and duns,
        And thresh and ply;
And hill-hid tides throb, throe on throe,
And meadow rivulets overflow,
And drops on gate bars hang in a row,
And rooks in families homeward go,
        And so do I.

Thomas Hardy (1840–1928)
Hardy is so much admired for his novels that it is easy to forget that he wrote some 250 poems as well. This one is particularly light and cheerful and was requested by Peggy Guttridge from Watford.

7.

Animals

TO THE CUCKOO
by William Wordsworth

O blithe New-comer! I have heard,
I hear thee and rejoice.
O Cuckoo! shall I call thee Bird,
Or but a wandering Voice?

While I am lying on the grass
Thy twofold shout I hear;
From hill to hill it seems to pass,
At once far off, and near.

Though babbling only to the vale
Of sunshine and of flowers,
Thou bringest unto me a tale
Of visionary hours.

Thrice welcome, darling of the Spring!
Even yet thou art to me
No bird, but an invisible thing,
A voice, a mystery;

The same whom in my school-boy days
I listened to; that cry
Which made me look a thousand ways
In bush, and tree, and sky.

To seek thee did I often rove
Through woods and on the green;
And thou wert still a hope, a love;
Still longed for, never seen.

And I can listen to thee yet;
Can lie upon the plain
And listen, till I do beget
That golden time again.

O blessèd Bird! the earth we pace
Again appears to be
An unsubstantial, faery place;
That is fit home for Thee!

The third and fourth lines of the first verse of this poem were once so often quoted that they even formed the basis of a Punch cartoon in the 1920s.

The picture featured two examiners walking through a park and the caption was their conversation:

First Examiner: *'O Cuckoo! shall I call thee Bird, Or but a wandering Voice?'*

Second Examiner: *'State the alternative preferred with reasons for your choice.'*

LITTLE TROTTY WAGTAIL
by John Clare

Little trotty wagtail, he went in the rain,
And tittering, tottering sideways he ne'er got straight again,
He stooped to get a worm, and looked up to get a fly,
And then he flew away ere his feathers they were dry.

Little trotty wagtail, he waddled in the mud,
And left his little footmarks, trample where he would.
He waddled in the water-pudge, and waggle went his tail,
And chirrup up his wings to dry upon the garden rail.

Little trotty wagtail, you nimble all about,
And in the dimpling water-pudge you waddle in and out;
Your home is nigh at hand, and in the warm pig-stye,
So, little Master Wagtail, I'll bid you a good-bye.

John Clare (1793–1864)
John Clare was one of the most remarkable poets of the nineteenth century.
Almost totally uneducated – he left school at the age of seven to work on his
father's farm – he became one of Britain's leading writers of verse and was
known as 'the Northamptonshire peasant poet'.

I LIKE LITTLE PUSSY
by Jane Taylor

I like little Pussy, her coat is so warm;
And if I don't hurt her she'll do me no harm.
So I'll not pull her tail, nor drive her away,
But Pussy and I very gently will play.

She shall sit by my side, and I'll give her some food;
And she'll love me because I am gentle and good.
I'll pat little Pussy and then she will purr,
And thus show her thanks for my kindness to her.

I'll not pinch her ears, nor tread on her paw,
Lest I should provoke her to use her sharp claw;
I never will vex her, nor make her displeased,
For Pussy can't bear to be worried or teased.

Jane Taylor (1783–1824)
Jane Taylor was a novelist and prolific writer of nursery rhymes, including Twinkle, Twinkle Little Star.
The above poem was requested by Jane Martin of Sheffield when her memory was jolted by a cat: 'I was visiting my grandchildren when their family cat climbed onto my knee and I suddenly found myself saying lines that I hadn't heard since my early school days around seventy years ago: "I love little pussy, her coat is so warm, and something something, do me no harm." Can you fill in the gaps please?'

THE NIGHTINGALE
by William Cowper

A nightingale, that all day long
Had cheered the village with his song,
Nor yet at eve his note suspended,
Nor yet when eventide was ended,
Began to feel, as well he might,
The keen demands of appetite;
When, looking eagerly around,
He spied far off, upon the ground,
A something shining in the dark,
And knew the glow-worm by his spark;
So, stooping down from hawthorn top,
He thought to put him in his crop.
The worm, aware of his intent,
Harangued him thus, right eloquent:
'Did you admire my lamp,' quoth he,
'As much as I your minstrelsy,
You would abhor to do me wrong,
As much as I to spoil your song;
For 'twas the self-same power divine,
Taught you to sing and me to shine;
That you with music, I with light,
Might beautify and cheer the night.'
The songster heard his short oration,
And warbling out his approbation,
Released him, as my story tells,
And found a supper somewhere else.

William Cowper (1731–1800)
William Cowper was a lawyer by training and an evangelical Christian by
vocation, but he attained his greatest successes as poet, hymn-writer and
letter-writer. His best-known work, which brought him great fame during his
own lifetime, was the long comic poem 'John Gilpin'.

THE LITTLE DOG-ANGEL
by Norah M Holland

High up in the courts of Heaven to-day
A little dog-angel waits,
With the other angels he will not play,
But he sits alone at the gates;
'For I know that my master will come,' says he:
'And when he comes, he will call for me.'

He sees the spirits that pass him by
As they hasten towards the throne,
And he watches them with a wistful eye
As he sits at the gates alone;
'But I know if I just wait patiently
That some day my master will come,' says he.

And his master, far on the earth below,
As he sits in his easy chair,
Forgets sometimes, and he whistles low
For the dog that is not there;
And the little dog-angel cocks his ears,
And dreams that his master's call he hears.

And I know, when at length his master waits
Outside in the dark and cold
For the hand of Death to ope the gates
That lead to those courts of gold,
The little dog-angel's eager bark
Will comfort his soul in the shivering dark.

Norah M Holland (1876–1925)
Norah M Holland was a Canadian poet of Irish ancestry who spent a year touring Ireland and England as a guest of her cousin, the poet W B Yeats.

The touching poem above was requested first by Mary Greenwood of Chelmsford, then asked for again by a surprising number of dog-lovers who had seen it in the paper and regretted not cutting it out to keep.

THE PRIEST AND THE MULBERRY TREE
by Thomas Love Peacock

Did you hear of the curate who mounted his mare,
And merrily trotted along to the fair?
Of creatures more tractable none ever heard:
In height of her speed would stop at a word;
But again with a word, when the curate said 'Hey',
She put forth her mettle and galloped away.

As near to the gates of the city he rode,
While the sun of September all brilliantly glowed,
The good priest discovered with eyes of desire,
A mulberry tree in a hedge of wild-brier;
On boughs long and lofty, in many a green shoot,
Hung, large, black, and glossy, the beautiful fruit.

The curate was hungry, and thirsty to boot;
He shrank from the thorns though but he longed for the fruit;
With a word he arrested his courser's keen speed,
And he stood up erect on the back of his steed;
On the saddle he stood while the creature stood still,
And he gathered the fruit till he took his good fill.

'Sure never,' he thought, 'was a creature so rare,
So docile, so true, as my excellent mare:
Lo, here now I stand,' and he gazed all around,
'As safe and as steady as if on the ground;
Yet how had it been, if some traveller this way
Had, dreaming no mischief, but chanced to cry 'HEY'?

He stood with his head in the mulberry tree,
And spoke out aloud in his fond reverie;
At the sound of the word the good mare made a push,
And down went the priest in the wild-brier bush.
He remembered too late, on his thorny green bed,
Much that well may be thought cannot wisely be said.

Thomas Love Peacock (1785–1866)
Thomas Love Peacock was a novelist, poet and particularly fine satirist who worked for most of his life in a very dull job at the East India Company.
*   The above verse, requested by Hugh T Clark of Newmarket, has a wonderfully appropriate rollicking rhythm to it.*

COYOTE
by Francis Bret Harte

Blown out of the prairie in twilight and dew,
Half bold and half timid, yet lazy all through;
Loath ever to leave, and yet fearful to stay,
He limps in the clearing, an outcast in gray.

A shade on the stubble, a ghost by the wall,
Now leaping, now limping, now risking a fall,
Lop-eared and large-jointed, but ever alway
A thoroughly vagabond outcast in gray.

Here, Carlo, old fellow, – he's one of your kind, –
Go, seek him, and bring him in out of the wind.
What! snarling, my Carlo! So even dogs may
Deny their own kin in the outcast in gray.

Well, take what you will – though it be on the sly,
Marauding or begging, – I shall not ask why,
But will call it a dole, just to help on his way
A four-footed friar in orders of gray!

Francis Bret Harte (1836–1902)
Francis Bret Hart was an American poet and author who specialised in writing about nineteenth-century pioneering life in California. After taking a wide variety of jobs, he was appointed US Consul in the town of Krefeld in Germany and then took a similar post in Glasgow. He later moved to London where he died. He is buried at St Peter's Church in Frimley, Surrey.

THE DONKEY
by G K Chesterton

When fishes flew and forests walked
And figs grew upon thorn,
Some moment when the moon was blood
Then surely I was born;

With monstrous head and sickening cry
And ears like errant wings,
The devil's walking parody
On all four-footed things.

The tattered outlaw of the earth,
Of ancient crooked will;
Starve, scourge, deride me: I am dumb,
I keep my secret still.

Fools! For I also had my hour;
One far fierce hour and sweet:
There was a shout about my ears,
And palms before my feet.

G K Chesterton (1874–1936)
Probably best remembered for his creation of the fictional detective Father
Brown, Chesterton was a prolific and witty novelist, short story writer and
essayist. He also wrote several hundred poems, of which 'The Donkey' is one
of the best known.

Mrs A Bell of Bristol requested this poem; she remembered learning the
poem at a small village school in East Yorkshire in the 1950s.

THE PLAINT OF THE CAMEL
by Charles Edward Carryl

Canary birds feed on sugar and seed,
Parrots have crackers to crunch;
And as for the poodles, they tell me the noodles
Have chickens and cream for their lunch.
But there's never a question
About my digestion –
Anything does for me!

Cats, you're aware, can repose in a chair,
Chickens can roost upon rails;
Puppies are able to sleep in a stable,
And oysters can slumber in pails.
But no one supposes
A poor Camel dozes –
Any place does for me!

Lambs are enclosed where it's never exposed,
Coops are constructed for hens;
Kittens are treated to houses well heated,
And pigs are protected by pens.
But a Camel comes handy
Wherever it's sandy –
Anywhere does for me!

People would laugh if you rode a giraffe
Or mounted the back of an ox;
It's nobody's habit to ride on a rabbit
Or try to bestraddle a fox.
But as for a Camel, he's
Ridden by families –
Any load does for me!

A snake is as round as a hole in the ground,
And weasels are wavy and sleek;
And no alligator could ever be straighter
Than lizards that live in a creek,
But a Camel's all lumpy
And bumpy and humpy –
Any shape does for me!

Charles Edward Carryl (1841–1920)
*For a man who wrote children's books and comic verse, Charles Carryl was,
surprisingly, a successful American businessman and stockbroker who held a
seat on the New York Stock Exchange for over thirty years. His first work was
called* Stock Exchange Primer *and the second was a children's fantasy serial
called* Davy and the Goblin.

A NIGHT WITH A WOLF
by Bayard Taylor

Little one come to my knee!
Hark how the rain is pouring
Over the roof in the pitch dark night,
And the winds in the woods a-roaring
Hush, my darling, and listen,
Then pay for the story with kisses;
Father was lost in the pitch-black night
In just such a storm as this is.

High on the lonely mountain
Where the wild men watched and waited;
Wolves in the forest, and bears in the bush,
And I on my path belated.
The rain and the night together
Came down, and the wind came after,
Bending the props of the pine tree roof
And snapping many a rafter.

I crept along in the darkness,
Stunned and bruised and blinded...
Crept to a fir with thick-set boughs,
And a sheltering rock behind it.
There, from the blowing and raining,
Crouching I sought to hide me;
Something rustled, two green eyes shone,
And a wolf lay down beside me.

Little one, be not frightened;
I and the wolf together,
Side by side through the long, long night,
Hid from the awful weather.
His wet fur pressed against me;
Each of us warmed the other;
Each of us felt in the stormy dark
That beast and man was brother.

And when the falling forest
No longer crashed in warning,
Each of us went from our hiding place
Forth in the wild wet morning.
Darling, kiss me in payment...
Hark! how the wind is roaring!
Father's house is a better place
When the stormy rain is pouring.

Bayard Taylor (1825–78)
Bayard Taylor was an American poet and writer, never happier than when he was travelling the world and subsequently lecturing about his experiences.

Herbert Eden from Ross-on-Wye requested the poem; he said he had been looking for it for over thirty years. 'I will be seventy-nine come Christmas and my father used to read this to me when I was a small boy.'

ON A FAVOURITE CAT,
DROWNED IN A TUB OF GOLDFISH
by Thomas Gray

'Twas on a lofty vase's side,
Where China's gayest art had dyed
The azure flowers that blow;
Demurest of the tabby kind,
The pensive Selima reclined,
Gazed on the lake below.

Her conscious tail her joy declared;
The fair round face, the snowy beard,
The velvet of her paws,
Her coat, that with the tortoise vies,
Her ears of jet, and emerald eyes,
She saw; and purr'd applause.

Still had she gazed; but 'midst the tide
Two angel forms were seen to glide,
The Genii of the stream:
Their scaly armour's Tyrian hue
Thro' richest purple to the view
Betray'd a golden gleam.

The hapless Nymph with wonder saw:
A whisker first and then a claw,
With many an ardent wish,
She stretch'd in vain to reach the prize.
What female heart can gold despise?
What Cat's averse to fish?

Presumptuous Maid! with looks intent
Again she stretch'd, again she bent,
　　Nor knew the gulf between.
(Malignant Fate sat by, and smiled.)
The slipp'ry verge her feet beguiled,
　　She tumbled headlong in.

Eight times emerging from the flood
She mew'd to ev'ry wat'ry god,
　　Some speedy aid to send.
No Dolphin came, no Nereid stirr'd:
Nor cruel Tom, nor Susan heard.
　　A Fav'rite has no friend!

From hence, ye Beauties, undeceived,
Know, one false step is ne'er retrieved,
　　And be with caution bold.
Not all that tempts your wand'ring eyes
And heedless hearts, is lawful prize;
　　Nor all that glisters, gold.

Thomas Gray (1716–71)
This is a delightful little piece by Thomas Gray, who is best known for his
'Elegy Written in a Country Churchyard'. Note the often-misquoted last line.
It's 'glisters' not 'glitters'. Mrs W Leather of Ryde, Isle of Wight, requested this
poem, telling us that she learnt it eighty-one years ago, when she was twelve
years old. 'I can remember quite a lot of it, but am completely lost after "The
Genii of the stream".'

THE TYGER
by William Blake

Tyger! Tyger! burning bright
In the forests of the night,
What immortal hand or eye
Could frame thy fearful symmetry?

In what distant deeps or skies
Burnt the fire of thine eyes?
On what wings dare he aspire?
What the hand dare seize the fire?

And what shoulder, and what art
Could twist the sinews of thy heart?
And when thy heart began to beat,
What dread hand? and what dread feet?

What the hammer? what the chain?
In what furnace was thy brain?
What the anvil? what dread grasp
Dare its deadly terrors clasp?

When the stars threw down their spears,
And watered heaven with their tears,
Did he smile his work to see?
Did he who made the Lamb make thee?

Tyger! Tyger! burning bright
In the forests of the night,
What immortal hand or eye
Dare frame thy fearful symmetry?

William Blake (1757–1827)
The spelling 'tyger' was already archaic when Blake wrote this poem for his Songs of Innocence and Experience *collection. He is believed to have opted for 'Tyger' rather than 'Tiger' because it conveyed a more frightening imagery.*

8.
Comic and
Humorous

AUNT TABITHA
by Oliver Wendell Holmes

Whatever I do, and whatever I say,
Aunt Tabitha tells me that isn't the way;
When she was a girl (forty summers ago)
Aunt Tabitha tells me they never did so.

Dear aunt! If I only would take her advice!
But I like my own way, and I find it so nice!
And besides, I forget half the things I am told;
But they all will come back to me – when I am old.

If a youth passes by, it may happen, no doubt,
He may chance to look in as I chance to look out;
She would never endure an impertinent stare,
It is horrid, she says, and I mustn't sit there.

A walk in the moonlight has pleasures, I own,
But it isn't quite safe to be walking alone;
So I take a lad's arm, – just for safety, you know,
But Aunt Tabitha tells me they didn't do so.

How wicked we are, and how good they were then!
They kept at arm's length those detestable men;
What an era of virtue she lived in! – But stay
Were the men all such rogues in Aunt Tabitha's day?

If the men were so wicked, I'll ask my papa
How he dared to propose to my darling mamma;
Was he like the rest of them? Goodness! Who knows?
And what shall I say if a wretch should propose?

I am thinking if aunt knew so little of sin,
What a wonder Aunt Tabitha's aunt must have been!
And her grand-aunt – it scares me – how shockingly sad.
That we girls of to-day are so frightfully bad!

A martyr will save us, and nothing else can;
Let me perish – to rescue some wretched young man!
Though when to the altar a victim I go,
Aunt Tabitha'll tell me she never did so!

Oliver Wendell Holmes (1809–94)
An American physician, writer and poet, Oliver Wendell Holmes was the
father of the even more famous Supreme Court Justice of the same name.
Gwen Watson from St Agnes, Cornwall requested the poem.

FATHER WILLIAM
by Lewis Carroll

'You are old, father William,' the young man said,
    'And your hair has become very white;
  And yet you incessantly stand on your head –
    Do you think, at your age, it is right?'

'In my youth,' father William replied to his son,
    'I feared it might injure the brain;
  But, now that I'm perfectly sure I have none,
    Why, I do it again and again.'

'You are old,' said the youth, 'as I mentioned before,
    And you've grown most uncommonly fat;
  Yet you turned a backsomersault in at the door –
    Pray what is the reason for that?'

'In my youth,' said the sage, as he shook his grey locks,
    'I kept all my limbs very supple
  By the use of this ointment – one shilling a box –
    Allow me to sell you a couple?'

'You are old,' said the youth, 'and your jaws are too weak
    For anything tougher than suet;
  Yet you finished the goose, with the bones and the beak –
    Pray, how did you manage to do it?'

'In my youth,' said his father, 'I took to the law,
    And argued each case with my wife;
  And the muscular strength, which it gave to my jaw,
    Has lasted the rest of my life.'

'You are old,' said the youth, 'one would hardly suppose
That your eye was as steady as ever;
Yet you balanced an eel on the end of your nose –
What made you so awfully clever?'

'I have answered three questions, and that is enough,'
Said his father. 'Don't give yourself airs!
Do you think I can listen all day to such stuff?
Be off, or I'll kick you down stairs.'

Lewis Carroll (1832–98)
*Like so many humorous verses by Lewis Carroll, this was a parody that
became far better known than the original. Carroll based the work on a poem
by Robert Southey called 'The Old Man's Comforts And How He Gained
Them', which began: 'You are old, Father William, the young man cried, The
few locks which are left are grey; You are hale, Father William, a hearty old
man, Now tell me the reason, I pray.'*

MEDDLESOME MATTY
by Ann Taylor

One ugly trick has often spoil'd
The sweetest and the best;
Matilda, though a pleasant child,
One ugly trick possess'd,
Which, like a cloud before the skies,
Hid all her better qualities.

Sometimes she'd lift the tea-pot lid,
To peep at what was in it,
Or tilt the kettle, if you did
But turn your back a minute.
In vain you told her not to touch,
Her trick of meddling grew so much.

Her grandmamma went out one day,
And by mistake she laid
Her spectacles and snuff-box gay
Too near the little maid;
'Ah! well,' thought she, 'I'll try them on,
As soon as grandmamma is gone.'

Forthwith she placed upon her nose
The glasses large and wide;
And looking round, as I suppose,
The snuff-box too she spied:
'Oh! what a pretty box is that;
I'll open it,' said little Matt.

'I know that grandmamma would say,
"Don't meddle with it, dear,"
But then, she's far enough away,
And no one else is near:
Besides, what can there be amiss
In opening such a box as this?'

So thumb and finger went to work
To move the stubborn lid,
And presently a mighty jerk
The mighty mischief did;
For all at once, ah! woeful case,
The snuff came puffing in her face.

Poor eyes, and nose, and mouth, beside
A dismal sight presented;
In vain, as bitterly she cried,
Her folly she repented.
In vain she ran about for ease;
She could do nothing now but sneeze.

She dash'd the spectacles away,
To wipe her tingling eyes,
And as in twenty bits they lay,
Her grandmamma she spies.
'Heyday! and what's the matter now?'
Says grandmamma, with lifted brow.

Matilda, smarting with the pain,
And tingling still, and sore,
Made many a promise to refrain
From meddling evermore.
And 'tis a fact, as I have heard,
She ever since has kept her word.

Ann Taylor (1782–1866)
Ann Taylor was the elder sister of Jane Taylor who has already appeared in this collection ('I Like Little Pussy', p.77). They collaborated on many children's books, but this verse is definitely Ann's work.

SWEET BABY BROTHER
Anonymous

A sweet little baby brother had come to live with Flo
And she wanted it brought to the table that it might eat and grow
'It must wait awhile,' said grandma in answer to her plea
'A little thing that hasn't teeth can't eat like you and me.'

'Why, hasn't it got teeth, grandma?' asked Flo in great surprise
'Oh my, but isn't it funny, no teeth, but nose and eyes.
I guess, after thinking gravely, they must have been forgot.
Can't we buy it some like grandpa's? I'd like to know why not.'

That afternoon to the table, with paper, pen and ink
Went Flo saying, 'don't you talk; if you do, you'll disturb my think.
I'm writing a letter Grandma, to send to Heaven tonight
And because it is very important, I want to get it right.'

At last the letter was finished, a wonderful thing to see
It was directed to God in Heaven, then Flo read it to me:
'Dear God, the baby you sent us was awfully nice and sweet
But because you forgot its toofies, the poor little thing can't eat.
So that's why I'm writing this letter, in order to let you know
So please come and finish our baby, that's all from Little Flo.'

*A very popular work, requested by many readers, but one of those
anonymous verses that has appeared in slightly different versions over the
years and nobody seems to know where it started or who wrote it.*

A MORTIFYING MISTAKE
by Anna Maria Pratt

I studied my tables over and over, and backward and
forward, too;
But I couldn't remember six times nine, and I didn't know
what to do,
Till sister told me to play with my doll, and not to bother
my head.
'If you call her "Fifty-four" for a while, you'll learn it by
heart,' she said.

So I took my favorite, Mary Ann (though I thought 'twas
a dreadful shame
To give such a perfectly lovely child such a perfectly
horrid name),
And I called her my dear little 'Fifty-four' a hundred times,
till I knew
The answer of six times nine as well as the answer of two
times two.

Next day Elizabeth Wigglesworth, who always acts
so proud,
Said, 'Six times nine is fifty-two,' and I nearly
laughed aloud!
But I wished I hadn't when teacher said, 'Now, Dorothy,
tell if you can.'
For I thought of my doll and – sakes alive! – I answered,
'Mary Ann!'

Anna Maria Pratt (dates unknown)
Anna Maria Pratt was a teacher in Cleveland, Ohio, who published her
Little Rhymes For Little People *in 1896.*

THE POBBLE WHO HAS NO TOES
by Edward Lear

The Pobble who has no toes
Had once as many as we;
When they said 'Some day you may lose them all;'
He replied 'Fish, fiddle-de-dee!'
And his Aunt Jobiska made him drink
Lavender water tinged with pink,
For she said 'The World in general knows
There's nothing so good for a Pobble's toes!'

The Pobble who has no toes
Swam across the Bristol Channel;
But before he set out he wrapped his nose
In a piece of scarlet flannel.
For his Aunt Jobiska said 'No harm
Can come to his toes if his nose is warm;
And it's perfectly known that a Pobble's toes
Are safe, – provided he minds his nose!'

The Pobble swam fast and well,
And when boats or ships came near him,
He tinkledy-blinkledy-winkled a bell,
So that all the world could hear him.
And all the Sailors and Admirals cried,
When they saw him nearing the further side –
'He has gone to fish for his Aunt Jobiska's
Runcible Cat with crimson whiskers!'

But before he touched the shore,
The shore of the Bristol Channel,
A sea-green porpoise carried away
His wrapper of scarlet flannel.
And when he came to observe his feet,
Formerly garnished with toes so neat,
His face at once became forlorn,
On perceiving that all his toes were gone!

And nobody ever knew,
From that dark day to the present,
Whoso had taken the Pobble's toes,
In a manner so far from pleasant.
Whether the shrimps, or crawfish grey,
Or crafty Mermaids stole them away –
Nobody knew: and nobody knows
How the Pobble was robbed of his twice five toes!

The Pobble who has no toes
Was placed in a friendly Bark,
And they rowed him back, and carried him up
To his Aunt Jobiska's Park.
And she made him a feast at his earnest wish
Of eggs and buttercups fried with fish, –
And she said 'It's a fact the whole world knows,
That Pobbles are happier without their toes!'

Edward Lear (1812–88)
Edward Lear was a master of nonsense verse, such as 'The Owl And The Pussy-Cat', and populariser of the Limerick. The above poem was requested by Diane Roberts from Cumbria who wrote, 'When I was a child in hospital having a toe removed, our class teacher read the class a poem "The Pobble Who Has No Toes". When I came back to school my nickname became Pobble.'

THE TWINS
by Henry Sambrooke Leigh

In form and feature, face and limb,
I grew so like my brother,
That folks got taking me for him,
And each for one another.

It puzzled all our kith and kin,
It reached a fearful pitch;
For one of us was born a twin,
Yet not a soul knew which.

One day, to make the matter worse,
Before our names were fixed,
As we were being washed by nurse,
We got completely mixed;

And thus, you see, by fate's decree,
Or rather nurse's whim,
My brother John got christened me,
And I got christened him.

This fatal likeness even dogged
My footsteps when at school,
And I was always getting flogged,
For John turned out a fool.

I put this question, fruitlessly,
     To everyone I knew,
'What would you do, if you were me,
     To prove that you were you?'

Our close resemblance turned the tide
     Of my domestic life,
For somehow, my intended bride
     Became my brother's wife.

In fact, year after year the same
     Absurd mistakes went on,
And when I died, the neighbors came
     And buried brother John.

Henry Sambrooke Leigh (1837–83)
Henry Sambrooke Leigh was a translator and writer of light verse, including the perfect couplet for slimmers: 'If you want to get slimmer, Diminish your dinner'.

JABBERWOCKY
by Lewis Carroll

'Twas brillg, and the slithy toves
Did gyre and gimble in the wabe
All mimsy were the borogoves,
And the mome raths outgrabe.

'Beware the Jabberwock, my son!
The jaws that bite, the claws that catch!
Beware the Jubjub bird, and shun
The frumious Bandersnatch.'

He took his vorpal sword in hand:
Long time the manxome foe he sought –
So rested he the Tumtum tree,
And stood awhile in thought.

And, as in uffish thought he stood,
The Jabberwock, with eyes of flame,
Came whiffling through the tulgey wood,
And burbled as it came!

One, two! One, two! And through and through
The vorpal blade went snicker-snack!
He left it dead, and with its head
He went galumphing back.

'And, has thou slain the Jabberwock?
Come to my arms, my beamish boy!
O frabjous day! Callooh! Callay!'
   He chortled his joy.

'Twas brillig and the slithy toves
Did gyre and gimble in the wabe
All mimsy were the borogoves
And the mome raths outgrabe.

Perhaps Carroll's most striking pieces of nonsense verse, this first appeared in Through the Looking-Glass and What Alice Found There, *published in 1872. Despite – or more likely because of – its inventive language, the first verse seems to have stuck in people's memories, but many have asked what happened after the mome raths outgrabe.*

ON WASHING DAY
by Fay Inchfawn

'I'm going to gran'ma's for a bit
My mother's got the copper lit;
An' piles of clothes are on the floor,
An' stream comes out the wash-house door;
An' Mrs Griggs has come, an' she
Is just as cross as she can be.
She's had her lunch, and ate a lot;
I saw her squeeze the coffeepot.
An' when I helped her make the starch,
She said: 'Now, miss, you just quick march!
What? Touch them soap-suds if you durst;
I'll see you in the blue-bag first!'
An' mother dried my frock, an' said:
'Come back in time to go to bed,'
I'm off to gran'ma's, for, you see,
At home, they can't put up with me.

But down at gran'ma's 'tis so nice.
If gran'ma's making currant-cake,
She'll let me put the ginger spice,
An' grease the tin, an' watch it bake;
An' then she says she thinks it fun
To taste the edges when it's done.

That's my gran'ma's house. Why, hip, hooray!
My gran'ma's got a washing day;
For gran'pa's shirts are on the line,
An' stockings, too – six, seven, eight, nine!
She'll let me help her. Yes, she'll tie
Her apron round to keep me dry;

An' on her little stool I'll stand
Up to the wash-tub. 'Twill be grand!
There's no cross Mrs Griggs to say,
'Young miss is always in the way.'
An' me and gran'ma will have tea
At dinner-time – just her an' me –
An' eggs, I 'spect, an' treacle rice.
My goodness! Won't it all be nice?

Gran'ma, I'll come spend the day,
'Cause mother finds me in the way.
Gran'ma, I'll peg the hankies out;
Gran'ma, I'll stir the starch about;
Gran'ma, I'm come, because, you see,
At home, they can't put up with me.

Elizabeth Rebecca Ward (dates unknown)
_We can find nothing about the author of this verse, except that Fay Inchfawn
was her pseudonym, and 'On Washing Day' comes from a collection
published in 1920 called_ The Verse-Book of a Homely Woman.

_Ann Steadman of Colchester requested the poem: 'My mother used to tell
parts of this poem to me as a small child many years ago. She couldn't
remember all of it, and I have forgotten even more. I would love to pass this
poem on to my grandchildren.'_

THE NIGHT WAS HORRIBLY DARK
by Susan Coolidge

The night was horribly dark,
The measles broke out in the Ark:
Little Japher, and Shem, and all the young Hams,
Were screaming at once for potatoes and clams.
And 'What shall I do,' said poor Mrs Noah,
'All alone by myself in this terrible shower:
I know what I'll do: I'll step down in the hold,
And wake up a lioness grim and old,
And tie her close to the children's door,
And give her a ginger-cake to roar
At the top of her voice for an hour or more;
And I'll tell the children to cease their din,
Or I'll let that grim old party in,
To stop their squeazles and likewise their measles.'
She practised this with the greatest success.
She was every one's grandmother, I guess.

Sarah Chauncey Woolsey (1835–1905)
*Susan Coolidge was the pen name of Sarah Chauncey Woolsey. She is best
known as the author of the Katy books, beginning with* What Katy Did *and*
What Katy Did Next. *The above verse comes from* What Katy Did At
School, *and appears in chapter six, in response to a challenge to write a
poem including the word 'measles' that answered the question, 'Who was the
grandmother of Invention?'*

9.
Children's Verse

THE UNSEEN PLAYMATE
by Robert Louis Stevenson

When children are playing alone on the green,
In comes the playmate that never was seen.
When children are happy and lonely and good,
The Friend of the Children comes out of the wood.

Nobody heard him and nobody saw,
His is a picture you never could draw,
But he's sure to be present, abroad or at home,
When children are happy and playing alone.

He lies in the laurels, he runs on the grass,
He sings when you tinkle the musical glass;
Whene'er you are happy and cannot tell why,
The Friend of the Children is sure to be by!

He loves to be little, he hates to be big,
'Tis he that inhabits the caves that you dig;
'Tis he when you play with your soldiers of tin
That sides with the Frenchman and never can win.

'Tis he, when at night you go off to your bed,
Bids you go to your sleep and not trouble your head;
For wherever they're lying, in cupboard or shelf,
'Tis he will take care of your playthings himself!

This is another poem from Robert Louis Stevenson's A Child's Garden of Verses and Underwoods *and was requested by Mrs B Booth of Sheffield.*

THE STAR
by Jane Taylor

Twinkle, twinkle, little star,
How I wonder what you are!
Up above the world so high,
Like a diamond in the sky.

When the blazing sun is gone,
When he nothing shines upon,
Then you show your little light,
Twinkle, twinkle, all the night.

Then the traveller in the dark,
Thanks you for your tiny spark:
He could not see which way to go,
If you did not twinkle so.

In the dark blue sky you keep,
And often through my curtains peep,
For you never shut your eye,
Till the sun is in the sky.

As your bright and tiny spark
Lights the traveller in the dark,
Though I know not what you are,
Twinkle, twinkle, little star.

We have already had one poem from each of the remarkable Taylor sisters.
Here is the one for which Jane is best known ... but how many of us realised
there was more than one verse?

THE DUEL
by Eugene Field

The gingham dog and the calico cat
Side by side on the table sat;
'Twas half-past twelve, and (what do you think!)
Nor one nor t'other had slept a wink!
The old Dutch clock and the Chinese plate
Appeared to know as sure as fate
There was going to be a terrible spat.
(I wasn't there; I simply state
What was told to me by the Chinese plate!)

The gingham dog went 'Bow-wow-wow!'
And the calico cat replied 'Me-ow!'
The air was littered, an hour or so,
With bits of gingham and calico,
While the old Dutch clock in the chimney place
Up with its hands before its face,
For it always dreaded a family row!
(Now mind: I'm only telling you
What the old Dutch clock declares is true!)

The Chinese plate looked very blue,
And wailed, 'Oh dear! What shall we do!'
But the gingham dog and the calico cat
Wallowed this way and tumbled that,
Employing every tooth and claw
In the awfullest way you ever saw –
And oh! how the gingham and calico flew!
(Don't fancy I exaggerate!
I got my news from the Chinese plate!)

Next morning where the two had sat
They found no trace of dog or cat;
And some folks think unto this day
That burglars stole the pair away!
But the truth about the cat and pup
Is this: they ate each other up!
Now what do you really think of that!
(The old Dutch clock, it told me so,
And that is how I came to know.)

Ms P Maher of Basingstoke requested this poem; she lamented not having made more effort to learn it at school in the 1940s. 'Why didn't I pay more attention in the classroom?' she bemoans. 'Now in my senior years, half-remembered lines are coming back to me. I hope you can trace the poem about the Gingham Dog and the Calico Cat, who side by side on the table sat. Or was it the fireplace? I remember they had a fight and at the end only pieces of material were left.'

MY SHADOW
by Robert Louis Stevenson

I have a little shadow that goes in and out with me,
And what can be the use of him is more than I can see.
He is very, very like me from the heels up to the head;
And I see him jump before me, when I jump into my bed.

The funniest thing about him is the way he likes to grow –
Not at all like proper children, which is always very slow;
For he sometimes shoots up taller like an India-rubber ball,
And he sometimes gets so little that there's none of him at all.

He hasn't got a notion of how children ought to play,
And can only make a fool of me in every sort of way.
He stays so close beside me, he's a coward you can see;
I'd think shame to stick to nursie as that shadow sticks to me!

One morning, very early, before the sun was up,
I rose and found the shining dew on every buttercup;
But my lazy little shadow, like an arrant sleepy-head,
Had stayed at home behind me and was fast asleep in bed.

This is another of Stevenson's marvellous poems for children, requested by Kenneth Golesworthy of Chessington, Surrey, who told us that he learnt it at school in the 1930s.

SOLOMON GRUNDY
Anonymous

Solomon Grundy,
Born on a Monday,
Christened on Tuesday,
Married on Wednesday,
Took ill on Thursday,
Grew worse on Friday,
Died on Saturday,
Buried on Sunday.
That was the end of
Solomon Grundy.

This is a verse with a mysterious history. James Orchard Halliwell-Phillipps first published it in 1842 in The Nursery Rhymes of England, *but it is not clear whether he wrote it. The verse appears to have been intended as a riddle (how did all that happen in one week?); the answer is that the events described take place on those days of the week, but in very different years.*

The name 'Solomon Grundy', incidentally, is believed to be a corruption of 'Salmagundi', a salad of cooked meats, anchovies, egg and lettuce.

THERE WAS A LITTLE WOMAN
by 'Mother Goose'

There was a little woman,
As I have heard tell,
She went to market
Her eggs for to sell;
She went to market
All on a market day,
And she fell asleep
On the king's highway.

There came by a pedlar,
His name was Stout,
He cut her petticoats
All around about;
He cut her petticoats
Up to her knees;
Which made the little woman
To shiver and sneeze.

When this little woman
Began to awake,
She began to shiver,
And she began to shake;
She began to shake and she began to cry,
Lawk a mercy on me,
This is none of I!

But if this be I,
As I do hope it be,
I have a little dog at home
And he knows me;
If it be I,
He'll wag his little tail,
And if it be not I
He'll loudly bark and wail!

Home went the little woman
All in the dark,
Up starts the little dog,
And he began to bark;
He began to bark,
And she began to cry,
Lawk a mercy on me,
This is none of I!

French writer Charles Perrault collected the original Mother Goose nursery rhymes in 1695, but many later collections in various languages also appeared under the name of Mother Goose. B Tissington of Inverness requested the poem.

THE LIMITATIONS OF YOUTH
by Eugene Field

I'd like to be a cowboy an' ride a fiery hoss
Way out into the big an' boundless west;
I'd kill the bears an' catamounts an' wolves I come across,
An' I'd pluck the bal' head eagle from his nest!
With my pistols at my side,
I would roam the prarers wide,
An' to scalp the savage Injun in his wigwam would I ride –
If I darst; but I darsen't!

I'd like to go to Afriky an' hunt the lions there,
An' the biggest ollyfunts you ever saw!
I would track the fierce gorilla to his equatorial lair,
An' beard the cannybull that eats folks raw!
I'd chase the pizen snakes
An' the 'pottimus that makes
His nest down at the bottom of unfathomable lakes –
If I darst; but I darsen't!

I would I were a pirut to sail the ocean blue,
With a big black flag aflyin' overhead;
I would scour the billowy main with my gallant pirut crew
An' dye the sea a gouty, gory red!
With my cutlass in my hand
On the quarterdeck I'd stand
And to deeds of heroism I'd incite my pirut band –
If I darst; but I darsen't!

And, if I darst, I'd lick my pa for the times that he's licked me!
I'd lick my brother an' my teacher, too!
I'd lick the fellers that call round on sister after tea,
An' I'd keep on lickin' folks till I got through!
You bet! I'd run away
From my lessons to my play,
An' I'd shoo the hens, an' tease the cat, an' kiss the girls all day –
If I darst; but I darsen't!

This is a deliciously misspelt verse, typical of the wondrous child-friendly humour of Eugene Field.

Tony Balcombe of Southampton requested the poem after recalling parts from his schooldays in the 1930s and wanting to pass it on to his own grandchildren.

THE SWING
by Robert Louis Stevenson

How do you like to go up in a swing,
Up in the air so blue?
Oh, I do think it the pleasantest thing
Ever a child can do!

Up in the air and over the wall,
Till I can see so wide,
Rivers and trees and cattle and all
Over the countryside?

Till I look down on the garden green,
Down on the roof so brown –
Up in the air I go flying again,
Up in the air and down!

The number of poems by Robert Louis Stevenson in this collection reflects the strong impression his works made on those who heard them at school, often long ago.

Sylvia Webster of Exeter told us this was the first poem she learnt at school over seventy years ago.

10.

Seasonal

SONG
by Sir William Watson

April, April,
Laugh thy girlish laughter;
Then, the moment after,
Weep thy girlish tears!
April, that mine ears
Like a lover greetest,
If I tell thee, sweetest,
All my hopes and fears,
April, April,
Laugh thy golden laughter,
But, the moment after,
Weep thy golden tears!

Sir William Watson (1858–1935)
Sir William Watson was renowned for his political and lyrical verse. William Pearson requested the poem after remembering only the first line, and having a vague feeling that it ends in tears.

APRIL RAIN
by Robert Loveman

It isn't raining rain to me,
It's raining daffodils;
In every dimpled drop I see
Wild flowers on the hills.
The clouds of gray engulf the day,
And overwhelm the town;
It isn't raining rain to me,
It's raining roses down.

It isn't raining rain to me,
But fields of clover bloom,
Where any buccaneering bee
May find a bed and room.
A health unto the happy,
A fig for him who frets –
It isn't raining rain to me,
It's raining violets.

Robert Loveman (1864–1923)
Robert Loveman was an American poet. The above verse brought back happy childhood memories for Joyce Whittaker from Barnoldswick, Lancashire.

THE COMING OF SPRING
by Mary Howitt

I am coming little maiden,
With the pleasant sunshine laden,
With the pollen for the bee,
With the blossom for the tree,
With the flower and with the leaf –
Till I come the time is brief.

I am coming, I am coming,
Hark the little bee is humming,
See the lark is soaring high
In the bright and sunny sky;
And the gnats are on the wing –
Little maiden now is Spring.

See the yellow catkins cover
All the slender willows over,
And on mossy banks so green
Starlike primroses are seen,
And their clustering leaves below
White and purple violets grow.

Hark! The little lambs are bleating,
And the cawing rooks are meeting
In the elms, a noisy crowd,
And all birds are singing loud,
And the first white butterfly
In the sun goes flitting by.

Little maiden look around thee,
Green and flowery fields surround thee;
Every little stream is bright,
All the orchard trees are white,
And each small and waving shoot
Has for thee sweet flower or fruit.

Turn thy eyes to earth and heaven,
Love, for thee the spring hath given,
Taught the birds their melodies,
Clothed the earth and cleared the skies.
For thy pleasure or thy food
Pour thy soul in gratitude,
So may thou midst blessings dwell,
Little maiden, fare thee well.

Mary Howitt (1799–1888)
Mary Howitt is best known as the author of 'The Spider And The Fly'
('Won't you come into my parlour...'). She and her husband William wrote
over 180 books between them, mostly on religious themes, but she also
translated Hans Anderson's tales into English, bringing them to a wider
audience than ever before.

OCTOBER
by Edward Thomas

The green elm with the one great bough of gold
Lets leaves into the grass slip, one by one, –
The short hill grass, the mushrooms small milk-white,
Harebell and scabious and tormentil,
That blackberry and gorse, in dew and sun,
Bow down to; and the wind travels too light
To shake the fallen birch leaves from the fern;
The gossamers wander at their own will.
At heavier steps than birds' the squirrels scold.
The rich scene has grown fresh again and new
As Spring and to the touch is not more cool
Than it is warm to the gaze; and now I might
As happy be as earth is beautiful,
Were I some other or with earth could turn
In alternation of violet and rose,
Harebell and snowdrop, at their season due,
And gorse that has no time not to be gay.
But if this be not happiness, – who knows?
Some day I shall think this a happy day,
And this mood by the name of melancholy
Shall no more blackened and obscured be.

Edward Thomas (1878–1917)
Edward Thomas was one of the best known of the English poets of his time.
He joined the Artists' Rifles when war broke out, though he was a mature
married man who had no need to enlist. He was killed in action at Arras on
April 9, 1917, soon after he arrived in France. The above poem is typical of
his work, a gentle evocation of the English countryside.

NOVEMBER
by Thomas Hood

No sun – no moon!
No morn – no noon!
No dawn – no dusk – no proper time of day –
No sky – no earthly view –
No distance looking blue –
No road – no street – no 't'other side this way' –
No end to any Row –
No indications where the Crescents go –
No top to any steeple –
No recognitions of familiar people –
No courtesies for showing 'em –
No knowing 'em!
No traveling at all – no locomotion –
No inkling of the way – no notion –
'No go' by land or ocean –
No mail – no post –
No news from any foreign coast –
No Park, no Ring, no afternoon gentility –
No company – no nobility –
No warmth, no cheerfulness, no healthful ease,
No comfortable feel in any member –
No shade, no shine, no butterflies, no bees,
No fruits, no flowers, no leaves, no birds –
November!

Thomas Hood (1799–1845)
This is a wonderfully witty account of all that is wrong with November, and was requested Miss M Axford of Burnham-on-Sea in Somerset: 'I remember a poem called November in which there was a line "No sun, no moon, no proper time of day". I don't know who wrote it, but I would like to read it again.'

THE TWO LITTLE STOCKINGS
by Sara Keables Hunt

Two little stockings hung side by side,
Close to the fireside broad and wide.
'Two?' said Saint Nick, as down he came,
Loaded with toys and many a game.
'Ho, ho!' said he, with a laugh of fun,
'I'll have no cheating, my pretty one.

'I know who dwells in this house, my dear,
There's only one little girl lives here.'
So he crept up close to the chimney place,
And measured a sock with a sober face;
Just then a wee little note fell out
And fluttered low, like a bird, about.

'Aha! What's this?' said he, in surprise,
As he pushed his specs up close to his eyes,
And read the address in a child's rough plan.
'Dear Saint Nicholas,' so it began,
'The other stocking you see on the wall
I have hung up for a child named Clara Hall.

'She's a poor little girl, but very good,
So I thought, perhaps, you kindly would
Fill up her stocking, too, to-night,
And help to make her Christmas bright.
If you've not enough for both stockings there,
Please put all in Clara's, I shall not care.'

Saint Nicholas brushed a tear from his eye,
And, 'God bless you, darling,' he said with a sigh;
Then softly he blew through the chimney high
A note like a bird's, as it soars on high,
When down came two of the funniest mortals
That ever were seen this side earth's portals.

'Hurry up,' said Saint Nick, 'and nicely prepare
All a little girl wants where money is rare.'
Then, oh, what a scene there was in that room!
Away went the elves, but down from the gloom
Of the sooty old chimney came tumbling low
A child's whole wardrobe, from head to toe.

How Santa Claus laughed, as he gathered them in,
And fastened each one to the sock with a pin;
Right to the toe he hung a blue dress, –
'She'll think it came from the sky, I guess,'
Said Saint Nicholas, smoothing the folds of blue,
And tying the hood to the stocking, too.

When all the warm clothes were fastened on,
And both little socks were filled and done,
Then Santa Claus tucked a toy here and there,
And hurried away to the frosty air,
Saying, 'God pity the poor, and bless the dear child
Who pities them, too, on this night so wild.'

The wind caught the words and bore them on high
Till they died away in the midnight sky;
While Saint Nicholas flew through the icy air,
Bringing 'peace and good will' with him everywhere.

Sara Keables Hunt (dates unknown)
Sara Keables Hunt was a children's writer of the late nineteenth century.
Judy Wise from Hull requested the poem, with a tale we have heard all too
often: 'My mum had a book, which unfortunately was loaned out and not
returned. It contained a poem that began "Two little stockings hung side by
side". I would love to read it again if possible.'

HANG UP THE BABY'S STOCKING
by Emily Huntington Miller

Hang up the baby's stocking:
Be sure you don't forget;
The dear little dimpled darling!
She ne'er saw Christmas yet;
But I've told her all about it,
And she opened her big blue eyes,
And I'm sure she understood it –
She looked so funny and wise.

Dear! what a tiny stocking!
It doesn't take much to hold
Such little pink toes as baby's
Away from the frost and cold.
But then for the baby's Christmas
It will never do at all;
Why, Santa wouldn't be looking
For anything half so small.

I know what will do for the baby.
I've thought of the very best plan:
I'll borrow a stocking of grandma,
The longest that ever I can;
And you'll hang it by mine, dear mother,
Right here in the corner, so!
And write a letter to Santa,
And fasten it on to the toe.

Write, 'This is the baby's stocking
That hangs in the corner here;
You never have seen her, Santa,
For she only came this year;
But she's just the blessedest baby!
And now, before you go,
Just cram her stocking with goodies,
From the top clean down to the toe.'

Emily Huntington Miller (1833–1913)
*The daughter of a Methodist minister in the United States, Miller helped edit a
children's magazine called* The Little Corporal *in which this verse first
appeared. It was requested by Mrs F Clark, from Alfreton, Derbyshire, who
wrote: 'In the early 1930s on Christmas Eve, my mother tucked me up in bed
with my stocking on the bed post and said a poem beginning, "Hang up the
baby's stocking, Be sure you don't forget." I am the oldest member of my
family and no one else has heard the poem. Please make Christmas special
for me if you can.'*

NOVEMBER SKIES
by John Freeman

Than these November skies
Is no sky lovelier. The clouds are deep;
Into their grey the subtle spies
Of colour creep,
Changing that high austerity to delight,
Till ev'n the leaden interfolds are bright.
And, where the cloud breaks, faint far azure peers
Ere a thin flushing cloud again
Shuts up that loveliness, or shares.
The huge great clouds move slowly, gently, as
Reluctant the quick sun should shine in vain,
Holding in bright caprice their rain.
And when of colours none,
Not rose, nor amber, nor the scarce late green,
Is truly seen, –
In all the myriad grey,
In silver height and dusky deep, remain
The loveliest,
Faint purple flushes of the unvanquished sun.

John Freeman (1880–1929)
John Freeman gave up a successful career in the insurance business in order to become a full-time writer. Michael Coombes, of Bridgnorth, Shropshire, requested this poem.

11.
War and Peace

BARBARA FRIETCHIE
by John Greenleaf Whittier

Up from the meadows rich with corn,
Clear in the cool September morn.
The clustered spires of Frederick stand
Green-walled by the hills of Maryland.
Round about them orchards sweep.
Apple and peach trees fruited deep,
Fair as a garden of the Lord
To the eyes of the famished rebel horde,

On that pleasant morn of the early fall
When Lee marched over the mountain wall,
Over the mountains, winding down,
Horse and foot into Frederick town.
Forty flags with their silver stars,
Forty flags with their crimson bars,
Flapped in the morning wind: the sun
Of noon looked down, and saw not one.

Tip rose old Barbara Frietchie then,
Bowed with her fourscore years and ten;
Bravest of all in Frederick town,
She took up the flag the men hauled down;
In her attic-window the staff she set,
To show that one heart was loyal yet.
Up the street came the rebel tread,
Stonewall Jackson riding ahead.

Under his slouched hat left and right
He glanced: the old flag met his sight.
'Halt!' – the dust-brown ranks stood fast;
'Fire!' – out blazed the rifle-blast.
It shivered the window, pane and sash;
It rent the banner with seam and gash.
Quick, as it fell, from the broken staff
Dame Barbara snatched the silken scarf;

She leaned far out on the window-sill,
And shook it forth with a royal will.
'Shoot, if you must, this old gray head,
But spare your country's flag,' she said.
A shade of sadness, a blush of shame,
Over the face of the leader came;
The nobler nature within him stirred
To life at that woman's deed and word:

'Who touches a hair of yon gray head
Dies like a dog! March on!' he said.
All day long through Frederick street
Sounded the tread of marching feet;
All day long that free flag tost
Over the heads of the rebel host.
Ever its torn folds rose and fell
On the loyal winds that loved it well;

And through the hill-gaps sunset light
Shone over it with a warm good-night.
Barbara Frietchie's work is o'er.
And the rebel rides on his raids no more.
Honor to her! and let a tear
Fall, for her sake, on Stonewall's bier.
Over Barbara Frietchie's grave,
Flag of freedom and union, wave!
Peace and order and beauty draw
Round thy symbol of light and law;
And ever the stars above look down
On thy stars below in Frederick town!

John Greenleaf Whittier (1807–92)
*We have had numerous requests for this remarkable poem by Whittier, which
has always been rather too long for publication in the* Daily Express, *and
which makes it all the more satisfying to include it in this collection. The story
is based on a true incident in the American Civil War. Barbara died in 1862
at the age of ninety-six years and is buried in the burial-ground of the
German Reformed Church in Frederick, Maryland.*

THE SOLDIER'S DREAM
by Thomas Campbell

Our bugles sang truce, for the night cloud had lower'd,
 And the sentinel stars set their watch in the sky;
And thousands had sunk on the ground overpower'd;
 The weary to sleep, and the wounded to die.

When resposing that night on my pallet of straw
 By the wolf-scaring faggot that guarded the slain,
At the dead of the night a sweet Vision I saw;
 And thrice ere on the morning I dreamt it again.

Methought from the battlefield's dreadful array
 Far, far, I had roam'd on a desolate track:
'Twas Autumn, – and sunshine arose on the way
To the home of my fathers, that welcomed me back.

I flew to the pleasant fields traversed so oft
 In life's morning march, when my bosom was young;
I heard my own mountain-goats bleating aloft,
And knew the sweet strain that the corn-reapers sung.

Then pledged we the wine-cup, and fondly I swore
From my home and my weeping friends never to part;
 My little ones kiss'd me a thousand times o'er,
And my wife sobb'd aloud in her fulness of heart.

'Stay – stay with us! rest! thou art weary and worn!'
 And fain was their war-broken soldier to stay;
But sorrow return'd with the dawning of morn,
 And the voice in my dreaming ear melted away.

Thomas Campbell was an influential and highly regarded Scottish poet who lived for most of his professional life in London and was one of the group who founded London University. Mrs E D Porter from Invernessshire requested this poem in memory of her late mother, who could recite it until a few months before her death at the age of ninety-five.

WILLIAM THE CONQUERER
Anonymous

William the Conqueror, 1066,
Said to his captains, 'I mean to affix
England to Normandy. Go out and borrow
Some bows and some arrows, we're starting tomorrow.'
So William went conquering hither and thither
Angles and Saxons were all of a dither.
He conquered so quickly you couldn't keep count
Of the counties he conquered, I think they amount
To ten, or a dozen, or even a score,
And I haven't a doubt he'd have conquered some more,
So full and so proud of his conquering tricks
Was William the Conquerer, 1066.
But death put an end to the tactics, thank Heaven,
Of William the Conquerer, 1087.

This verse came in response to a heartfelt request from Mrs Pat Davidson of Manchester: 'My sister and I learnt a verse about William the Conquerer at Gorse Hill Primary School, Stretford, but we are unable to remember the whole of it, nor can we find anyone else who knows it. Please, please can you help; it is driving me crazy trying to remember it.'

ENGLAND AND HER COLONIES
by William Watson

She stands, a thousand-wintered tree
By countless morns impearled;
Her broad roots coil beneath the sea,
Her branches sweep the world;
Her seeds, by careless winds conveyed,
Clothe the remotest strand
With forest from her scatterings made,
New nations fostered in her shade,
And linking land with land.

O ye by wandering tempest sown
'Neath every alien star,
Forget not whence the breath was blown
That wafted you afar!
For ye are still her ancient seed
On younger soil let fall
Children of Britain's island-breed,
To whom the Mother in her need
Perchance may one day call.

William Watson (1858–1935)
Written in 1903, this is a poem from the days of Empire, praising England's place in the world. Cath Paxton of Eyemouth requested it, having remembered reciting it at a shool concert in connection with the Festival of Britain in 1951.

THE SIEGE OF BELGRADE
by Alaric Alexander Watts

An Austrian army, awfully arrayed,
Boldly by battery beseiged Belgrade.
Cossack commanders cannonading come,
Dealing destruction's devastating doom.
Every endeavour engineers essay,
For fame, for fortune fighting – furious fray!
Generals 'gainst generals grapple – gracious God!
How honors Heaven heroic hardihood!
Infuriate, indiscriminate in ill,
Kindred kill kinsmen, kinsmen kindred kill.
Labor low levels longest, loftiest lines;
Men march 'mid mounds, 'mid moles, 'mid muderous mines;
Now noxious, noisy numbers nothing, naught
Of outward obstacles, opposing ought;
Poor patriots, partly purchased, partly pressed,
Quite quaking, quickly 'Quarter! Quarter!' quest.
Reason returns, religious right redounds,
Suwarrow stops such sanguinary sounds.
Truce to thee, Turkey! Triumph to thy train,
Unwise, unjust, unmerciful Ukraine!
Vanish vain victory! vanish, victory, vain!
Why wish we warfare? Wherefore welcome were
Xexes, Ximenes, Xanthus, Xavier?
Yield, yield, ye youths! ye yeomen, yield your yell!
Zeus', Zarpater's, Zoroaster's zeal,
Attracting all, arms against acts appeal!

Alaric Alexander Watts (1797–1864)
Alaric Alexander Watts was a poet, journalist and newspaper editor who served a brief sentence in a debtors' prison after founding rather too many unsuccessful publications. Louis Siedle requested the poem: 'Many years ago, I was talking with an aunt about alliteration in literature and she quoted the first few lines of a poem of around the Crimean War period, which she had come across at school. I've been trying for years to find the whole poem.'

DEATH THE LEVELLER
by James Shirley

The glories of our blood and state
Are shadows, not substantial things;
There is no armour against Fate;
Death lays his icy hand on kings:
Sceptre and Crow
Must tumble down,
And in the dust be equal made
With the poor crooked scythe and spade.

Some men with swords may reap the field,
And plant some fresh laurels where they kill:
But their strong nerves at last must yield;
They tame but one another still:
Early or late
They stoop to fate
And must give up their murmuring breath
When they, pale captives, creep to death.

The garlands wither on your brow,
Then boast no more your mighty deeds!
Upon Death's purple alter now
See where the victor-victim bleeds.
Your heads must come
To the cold tomb:
Only the actions of the just
Smell sweet and blossom their dust.

James Shirley (1596–1666)
James Shirley has been called the 'Last of the Elizabethan Poets' and is said to have died from 'fright and exposure' when the Great Fire of London raged in 1666. Mr F Leeves of Five Ashes, East Sussex, requested the poem, having remembered only the second half of the first verse from his schooldays.

THE DESTRUCTION OF SENNACHERIB
by George Gordon, Lord Byron

The Assyrian came down like a wolf on the fold,
And his cohorts were gleaming in purple and gold;
And the sheen of their spears was like stars on the sea,
When the blue wave rolls nightly on deep Galilee.

Like the leaves of the forest when Summer is green,
That host with their banners at sunset were seen:
Like the leaves of the forest when Autumn hath blown,
That host on the morrow lay withered and strown.

For the Angel of Death spread his wings on the blast,
And breathed in the face of the foe as he passed;
And the eyes of the sleepers waxed deadly and chill,
And their hearts but once heaved, and for ever grew still!

And there the steed with his nostril all wide,
But through it there rolled not the breath of his pride;
And the foam of his gasping lay white on the turf,
And cold as the spray of the rock-beating surf.

And there lay the rider distorted and pale,
With the dew on his brow, and the rust on his mail:
And the tents were all silent, the banners alone,
The lances unlifted, the trumpet unblown.

The the widows of Ashur are loud in their wail,
And the idols are broke in the temple of Baal;
And the might of the Gentile, unsmote by the sword,
Hath melted like snow in the glance of the Lord!

---

*This is Byron's powerful re-telling of a story found in the Second Book of
Kings (chapters eighteen and nineteen) of the siege of Jerusalem by the armies
of Sennacherib and the intervention of the Angel of Death.*

PIBROCH OF DONUIL DHU
by Sir Walter Scott

Pibroch of Donuil Dhu
Pibroch of Donuil
Wake thy wild voice anew,
Summon Clan Conuil.
Come away, come away,
Hark to the summons!
Come in your war-array,
Gentles and commons.

Come from deep glen, and
From mountain so rocky;
The war-pipe and pennon
Are at Inverlocky.
Come every hill-plaid, and
True heart that wears one;
Come every steel blade, and
Strong hand that bears one.

Leave untended the herd,
The flock without shelter;
Leave the corpse uninterr'd,
The bride at the altar;
Leave the deer, leave the steer,
Leave nets and barges:
Come with your fighting gear,
Broadswords and targes.

Comes as the winds come when
Forests are rended,
Come as the waves come when
Navies are stranded:
Faster come, faster come,
Faster and faster,
Chief, vassal, page, and groom,
Tenant and master.

Fast they come, fast they come –
See how they gather!
Wide waves the eagle plume
Blended with heather.
Cast your plaids, draw your blades,
Forward each man set!
Pibroch of Donuil Dhu,
Knell for the onset!

Sir Walter Scott (1771–1832)
*Also known as 'The Gathering Song of Donald the Black', this poem tells of
Donald Balloch, who in 1431 launched from the Isles with great force,
invaded Lochaber, and at Inverlochy defeated and put to flight the Earls of
Mar and Caithness, despite being outnumbered. A Pibroch is a piper or a
marching song.*

WAR SONG OF THE SARACENS
by James Elroy Flecker

We are they who come faster than fate: we are they who
ride early or late:
We storm at your ivory gate: Pale Knights of the sunset,
beware!
Not in silk nor in samet we lie, not in curtained
solemnity die
Among women who chatter and cry, and children who
mumble a prayer.
But we sleep by the ropes of the camp, and we rise with
a shout, and we tramp
With the sun or the moon for a lamp, and the spray of the
wind in our hair.

From the lands, where the elephants are, to the forts of
Merou and Balghar,
Our steel we have brought and our star to shine on the
ruins of Rum.
We have marched from the Indus to Spain, and by God
we will go there again;
We have stood on the shore of the plain where the Waters
of Destiny boom.
A mart of destruction we made at Jalula where men
were afraid,
For death was a difficult trade, and the sword was a
broker of doom;

And the spear was a Desert Physician who cured not a
few of ambition,
And drave not a few to perdition with medicine
bitter and strong:
And the shield was a grief to the fool and as bright as a
desolate pool,
And as straight as the rock of Stamboul when their cavalry
thundered along;
For the coward was drowned with the brave when our battle
sheered up like a wave,
And the dead to the desert we gave, and the glory of God in
our song.

James Elroy Flecker (1884–1915)
Despite a tragically early death from tuberculosis, James Elroy Flecker
established himself as a leading British writer in the years before the First
World War. An excerpt from his poem 'The Golden Journey to Samarkand'
can be seen inscribed on the clock tower of the barracks of the British Army's
22nd SAS regiment in Hereford.

KUBLA KHAN
by Samuel Taylor Coleridge

In Xanadu did Kubla Khan
A stately pleasure-dome did decree:
Where Alph, the sacred river, ran
Through caverns measureless to man
Down to a sunless sea.

So twice five miles of fertile ground
With walls and towers were girdled round:
And there were gardens bright with sinuous rills,
Where blossomed many an incense-burning tree;
And here were forests ancient as the hills,
Enfolding sunny spots of greenery.

But oh! that deep romantic chasm which slanted
Down the green hill athwart a cedarn cover!
A savage place! as holy and enchanted
As e'er beneath a waning moon was haunted
By woman wailing for her demon-lover!
And from this chasm, with ceaseless turmoil seething,
As if this earth in fast thick pants were breathing,
A mighty fountain momently was forced:
Amid whose swift half-intermitted burst
Huge fragments vaulted like rebounding hail,
Or chaffy grain beneath the thresher's flail:
And 'mid these dancing rocks at once and ever
It flung up momently the sacred river.
Five miles meandering with a mazy motion
Through wood and dale the sacred river ran,
Then reached the caverns measureless to man,
And sank in tumult to a lifeless ocean:
And 'mid this tumult Kubla heard from far
Ancestral voices prophesying war!

The shadow of the dome of pleasure
Floated midway on the waves;
Where was heard the mingled measure
From the fountain and the caves.
It was a miracle of rare device,
A sunny pleasure-dome with caves of ice!

A damsel with a dulcimer
In a vision once I saw:
It was an Abyssinian maid,
And on her dulcimer she played,
Singing of Mount Abora.
Could I revive within me
Her symphony and song,
To such a deep delight 'twould win me,
That with music loud and long,
I would build that dome in air,
That sunny dome! those caves of ice!
And all who heard should see them there,
And all should cry, Beware! Beware!
His flashing eyes, his floating hair!
Weave a circle round him thrice,
And close your eyes with holy dread,
For he on honey-dew hath fed,
And drunk the milk of Paradise.

Samuel Taylor Coleridge (1772–1834)
This is a mystical but often requested verse by Coleridge, who claimed that it was inspired by an opium-induced dream, but that a person from Porlock interrupted the composition, and that the second half was never written. Its imagery explores the tense boundaries between perfect peace and tumult.

Index of first lines

Index of poets

About the Author

William Hartston has been writing for the *Daily Express* since 1998, contributing the daily Beachcomber column, as well as a variety of columns on useless information (including the daily Ten Things You Didn't Know About...), the Saturday Briefing page, and, of course, Forgotten Verse. He also contributes a number of the paper's puzzles, an expertise he attributes to a wasted youth. He has written extensively on the game of chess, and was British Chess Champion in 1973 and 1975.

Has this book brought back memories of any verse you may have learnt at school or come across later in life that you would like us to try to track down? We cannot promise to find it for you, or to reply to every letter and e-mail, but every request we receive is given consideration. Even when they are not published in the *Daily Express*, we often send personal replies, too – especially when prevented by copyright law from publishing them, or when the poems asked for have already appeared in the paper.

So if you do have any snippets of verse that need to be completed, just write to: Forgotten Verse, Daily Express, 10 Lower Thames Street, London EC3R 6EN, or e-mail william.hartston@express.co.uk and we'll do the best we can.

You will also find a Forgotten Verse section on our website at www.express.co.uk where, as well as offering a daily verse, we are building up a searchable archive of poems, including both those which have been published in the newspaper and many that have not.